THE ANCIENT MUSIC

OF

Arranged for the

PIANO FORTE.

To which is prefixed

A DISSERTATION ON

THE IRISH HARP AND HARPERS,

INCLUDING AN ACCOUNT OF THE

OLD MELODIES OF IRELAND.

BY EDWARD BUNTING.

Dublin:

HODGES AND SMITH.

1840.

The Ancient Music of Ireland

Arranged for Piano

Prefaced by the author's complete
"A Dissertation on the Irish Harp and Harpers,
including an Account of the Old Melodies of Ireland" (1840)

Edward Bunting

DOVER PUBLICATIONS, INC.
Mineola, New York

Edward Bunting (1773–1843) was the first systematic collector of Irish folksongs and a leading musician in Belfast. Of particular significance was the meeting of harpers in Belfast in July 1792 at which he acted as scribe, notating the performances of traditional players. He thus preserved this music from oblivion, becoming virtually the only source for the manners and customs of that ancient tradition.

Bibliographical Note

This Dover edition, first published in 2000, is a complete, unabridged republication of the work originally published by Hodges and Smith, Dublin, 1840. Two harp drawings have been repositioned between pages 40–41, with a footnote reference newly added to page 43.

We are grateful to Stuart Isacoff for bringing this important work to our attention.

International Standard Book Number: 0-486-41376-4

Manufactured in the United States of America
Dover Publications, Inc., 31 East 2nd Street, Mineola, N.Y. 11501

CONTENTS.

Page.

PREFACE, ... 1

Chapter I. OF THE CHARACTERISTICS OF IRISH MELODY, ... 13

II. OF THE METHOD OF PLAYING, AND MUSICAL VOCABULARY OF THE OLD IRISH HARPERS, ... 18

III. OF THE ANTIQUITY OF THE HARP AND BAGPIPE IN IRELAND, ... 37

IV. OF THE VARIOUS EFFORTS TO REVIVE THE IRISH HARP, ... 60

V. ANECDOTES OF THE MORE DISTINGUISHED HARPERS OF THE LAST TWO CENTURIES, ... 67

VI. NOTICES OF THE MORE REMARKABLE MELODIES AND PIECES OF THE COLLECTION, ... 82

INDEX TO THE AIRS, ... i

ANCIENT IRISH MELODIES ADAPTED TO THE PIANO FORTE.

PREFACE.

WHATEVER differences of opinion may exist as to the high degree of early civilization and national glory laid claim to by the Irish people, it has never been questioned that, in the most remote times, they had at least a national music peculiar to themselves, and that their bards and harpers were eminently skilful in its performance.

The investigation of our civil and military antiquities, notwithstanding all the doubts which beset the inquiry, has always been esteemed an honourable and patriotic employment, and many ingenious and worthy men have in this way obtained the applauses of the learned, and the approbation of their own countrymen. It is submitted then, that if such rewards attend speculations on the uncertain, or at least debateable matters connected with the early condition of society among our ancestors, some share of public approval and encouragement may fairly be expected for an attempt to elucidate a subject which, of all those involved in Irish history, is the one most capable of being handled with certainty and precision.

Poems and histories, when orally delivered, will, from time to time, be corrupted and interpolated. Thus, of all the poems attributed to Ossian, it is now impossible to say whether any, or any part even, be undoubtedly genuine. So also, but in a higher degree, with regard to songs. The words of the popular songs of every country vary according to the several provinces and districts in which they are sung : as, for example, to the popular air of *Aileen-a-Roon,* we here find as many different sets of words as there are counties in one of our provinces. But the case is totally different with music. A strain of music, once impressed on the popular ear, never varies. It may be made the vehicle of many different sets of words, but they are adapted to *it,* not it to *them,* and it will no more alter its character on their account than a ship will change the number of its masts an account of an alteration in the nature of its lading. For taste in music is so universal, especially among country people, and in a pastoral age, and airs are so easily, indeed, in many instances, so intuitively acquired, that when a melody has once been divulged in any district, a criterion is immediately established in almost every ear ; and this criterion being the more infallible in proportion as it requires less effort in judging, we have thus, in all directions, and at all times, a tribunal of the utmost accuracy and of unequalled impartiality (for it is unconscious of the exercise of its own authority) governing the musical traditions of the people, and preserving the native airs and melodies of every country, in their integrity, from the earliest periods. It is thus that changes in the actual frame and structure of our melodies have never been attempted, unless on the introduction of the altered tunes for the first time amongst those who had never heard them in their original state ; as in the instance of Sir John Stevenson's supposed emendations of the Irish melodies on their first introduction to that extended auditory procured for them by the excellence of Mr. Moore's accompanying poetry ; and thus it is, that so long as the musical collector or antiquary confines his search to the native districts of the tunes he seeks for, he may always be certain of the absolute and unimpeachable authenticity of every note he procures.

Were it not for this provision for the transmission of tunes in a perfect state from the earliest times, there would be no such thing (at least in our age of the world) as musical antiquity, or the means of judging from musical remains of the genius and sentiment, and, through them, of the mental refinement and social progress of our remote ancestors : for musical notation is of comparatively recent origin, and without it we have nothing but this tradition to depend on. But, there being this provision made for the perpetuation of tunes, musical antiquity becomes, in its way, of just as much importance as civil or military, or (apart from doctrinal differences) as ecclesiastical antiquity. For the aim of all is to realize former times, so as to bring us acquainted with our ancestors ; and if, towards forming that acquaintance, it be satisfactory to ascertain their exploits in war, or their progress in the arts of building and tillage, it surely must afford an equal share of pleasure to the reflective inquirer to become acquainted with the men themselves, and with their general turn of mind and sentiment in the very notes and cadences by which they gave expression to their ruling passions.

The hope of being thus enabled, by reviving the national music, to place himself in the same rank with those worthy Irishmen whose labours have from time to time sustained the reputation of the country for a native literature, had, the Editor admits, no inconsiderable share in determining him on making the study and preservation of our Irish melodies the main business of his long life, and, he is free to confess, the same hope still animates him in giving these, the last of his labours, to the public. But what at first incited him to the pursuit, and what has chiefly kept alive the adour with which, for nearly fifty years, he has prosecuted it, was and is a strong innate love of these delightful strains for their own sake, a love for them which neither the experience of the best music of other countries, nor the control of a vitiated public taste, nor the influence of advancing years, has ever been able to alter or diminish.

The occasion which first confirmed the Editor in this partiality for the airs of his native country, was the great meeting of the Harpers at Belfast, in the year 1792. Before this time there had been several similar meetings at Granard, in the county of Longford, which had excited a surprising degree of interest in Irish music through that part of the country. The meeting at Belfast was, however, better attended than any that had yet taken place, and its effects were more permanent, for it kindled an enthusiasm throughout the North which burns bright in some warm and honest hearts to this day. All the best of the old class of harpers—a race of men then nearly extinct, and now gone for ever—Denis Hempson, Arthur O'Neill, Charles Fanning, and seven others, the least able of whom has not left his like behind, were present. Hempson, who realized the antique picture drawn by Cambrensis and Galilei, for he played with long crooked nails, and in his performance, "the tinkling of the small wires under the deep notes of the bass" was peculiarly thrilling, took the attention of the Editor with a degree of interest which he never can forget. He was the only one who played the very old—the aboriginal—music of the country ; and this he did in a style of such finished excellence as persuaded the Editor that the praises of the old Irish harp in Cambrensis, Fuller, and others, instead of being, as the detractors of the country are fond of asserting, ill-considered and indiscriminate, were in reality no more than a just tribute to that admirable instrument and its then professors. But, more than any thing else, the conversation of Arthur O'Neill, who, although not so absolute a harper as Hempson, was more a man of the world, and had travelled in his calling over all parts of Ireland, won and delighted him. All that the genius of later poets and romance writers has feigned of the wandering minstrel, was realized in this man. There was no house of any note in the north of Ireland, as far as Meath on the one hand, and Sligo on the other, in which he was not well known and eagerly sought after. Carolan had been his immediate predecessor, and those who have taken any interest in the life of the elder minstrel will readily recognize the names of Charles O'Conor of Belanagar, Toby Peyton of Lisduff, James Irwin of Streamstown,[a]

[a] "I am totally at a loss," says O'Neill, (*MS. penes the Editor,*) "to describe that gentleman's manner of living at his own house, and amongst his tenantry. He had an ample fortune, and was passionately fond of music. He had four sons and three daughters, who were all proficients ; no instrument was unknown to them. There

Mrs. Crofton of Longford, Con O'Donnell of Larkfield, Squire Jones of Moneyglass—not to detain the reader with a longer enumeration—all of whom are to be found among the list of O'Neill's friends and entertainers. He had also, when a youth, been through the South, where his principal patron was the famous Murtagh Oge O'Sullivan of Bearhaven, a man who led quite the life of an old Irish chieftain, and whose memory is still vividly preserved in the lays and traditions of the county of Cork. O'Neill was of the great Tyrone family, and prided himself on his descent, and on supporting, to some extent, the character of a gentleman harper. Although blind from his youth, he possessed a surprising capacity for the observation of men and manners. He had been the intimate friend of Acland Kane, who had played before the Pretender, the Pope, and the King of Spain. He himself had played on Brian Boru's harp, strung for the occasion, through the streets of Limerick in the year 1760; in a word, he was a man whose conversation was enough to enamour any one of Irish music, much more one so enthusiastic in *every thing Irish* as the Editor.

Animated by the countenance and assistance of several townsmen of congenial taste and habits, of whom his excellent friend Doctor James M'Donnell is now, alas! the only survivor, and assisted, to a great extent, by O'Neill and the other harpers present on this memorable occasion, the Editor, immediately after the termination of the meeting, commenced forming his first collection. For this purpose he travelled into Derry and Tyrone, visiting Hempson, after his return to Magilligan in the former county, and spending a good part of the summer about Ballinascreen and other mountain districts in the latter, where he obtained a great number of admirable airs from the country people. His principal acquisitions were, however, made in the province of Connaught, whither he was invited by the celebrated Richard Kirwan of Cregg, the philosopher, and founder of the Royal Irish Academy, who was himself an ardent lover of the native music, and who was of such influence in that part of the country, as procured the Editor a ready opportunity of obtaining tunes both from high and low. Having succeeded beyond his expectations, he returned to Belfast, and in the year 1796 produced his first volume, containing sixty-six native Irish airs never before published.

Before this time there had been but three attempts of this nature: one by Burke Thumoth, in 1720, another by Neill of Christ Churchyard, soon after, and a third by Carolan's son, patronized by Dean Delany, about 1747. In all these, the arrangement was calculated rather for the flute or violin than for a keyed instrument, so that the tunes were

was at one time a meeting in his house of forty-six musicians, who played in the following order: the three Miss Irwins at the piano; myself at the harp; gentlemen flutes, six; gentlemen violincellos, two; common pipers, ten; gentlemen fiddlers, twenty; gentlemen clarionets, four."

to a great extent deprived of their peculiar character; and, as they were deficient in arrangement, so were they meagre in extent. On the whole, the Editor may safely say that his publication above alluded to, was the first and only collection of genuine Irish harp music given to the world up to the year 1796.

The *eclat* of the Granard and Belfast Meetings, joined to the success of this publication, which was one chief cause also of the establishment of the Irish Harp Society in Belfast, had the effect of rendering our native music rather fashionable, and the Editor was gratified to find that the tunes which had thus for the first time been brought before the public, were soon adopted as vehicles for the most beautiful popular songs that have perhaps ever been composed by any lyric poet. "The Twisting of the Rope," "The Brown Thorn," "The Fox's Sleep," and many other airs too numerous to particularize in this place,[a] now assumed a new dress—one, indeed, in point of poetic diction and classical ornament infinitely more elegant than they had ever worn before—under the hands of Mr. Moore; but the Editor saw with pain, and still deplores the fact, that in these new Irish melodies, the work of the poet was accounted of so paramount an interest, that the proper order of song writing was in many instances inverted, and, instead of the words being adapted to the tune, the tune was too often adapted to the words, a solecism which could never have happened had the reputation of the writer not been so great as at once to carry the tunes he deigned to make use of altogether out of their old sphere among the simple and tradition-loving people of the country—with whom, in truth, many of the new melodies, to this day, are hardly suspected to be themselves.

Notwithstanding the chagrin with which the Editor saw the old national music, which it had been, and still is, his ambition to preserve in its integrity, thus unworthily handled and sent abroad throughout the whole world in a dress so unlike its native garb, he did not relax in his efforts to procure and publish as many more airs as he could collect in repeated journeys through all parts of the country, where he had any expectation of finding the old music preserved, but chiefly through Ulster and Connaught; even though in doing so he had no other prospect than that of seeing these fruits of his labour caught up as soon as they appeared, to be sent forth again in similar disguises. He accordingly published his second volume, containing seventy-five additional tunes, with a dissertation on the Irish harp prefixed, in 1809. This volume, like the first, afforded a copious fund of new melodies, of which the song-writers of the day eagerly and largely availed themselves. The beauty of Mr. Moore's

[a] In fact, eleven out of the sixteen airs in Mr. Moore's first number were taken immediately from the volume above-mentioned.

words, in a great degree atones for the violence done by the musical arranger to any of the airs which he has adopted, (and they are even more numerous than in the instance of the first volume,) but there are others who have spoiled several fine airs given in this and the former publication, without even equalling, much less improving on, the rude accompanying lyrics of the country.

In preparing the materials of this second publication, the Editor had occasion frequently to visit Hempson, who was now bedridden, being over 100 years old. From him he not only procured many of the best and most ancient pieces in the whole collection, but learned also his peculiar mode of playing and fingering—the identical manner described by Cambrensis—together with a great number of the terms of musical science used among the old Irish harpers, and of which he had already got a large collection from O'Neill. Being in possession of these technical terms, and having learned their practical illustration from the very wires of Hempson's harp, that "Queen of Music," as it was called in those days, he began to entertain the hope of being able to do something more for Irish music than merely to collect and publish its remains as so many *disjecta membra citharæ ;* and, with this object in view, he has endeavoured for the last thirty years not only to procure all the genuine airs hitherto unpublished, and to arrange them in true harp style, as they may have been played by the Scotts, O'Cahans, and Connallons of former times, and as they would now be played by Hempson if he were still alive ; but also, so to classify them as to render the whole series subservient to an investigation of the principles and history of our native music, an investigation which he is well aware he can only conduct a comparatively short distance, but one in which to make any progress is worth so much, that, if he has succeeded in effecting ever so little, he counts the time and labour he has spent in the pursuit, as nothing.

The object, then, of the present publication chiefly is to give the remaining airs of the collection arranged in true harp style, for the piano forte, accompanied by a practical digest of ancient Irish musical science. The Editor's chief aim throughout has been to guard the primitive air with a religious veneration. To this he has made everything else subordinate ; and, finding that the adaptation of words, even of those to which the airs have been sung for generations back, being embarrassed by a defective accompaniment, interferes with the purity of their arrangement, he has, in almost every instance, given the music alone.

The entire number of airs is upwards of 150. Of these, considerably more than 120 are now for the first time published, the remainder being sets much superior to those already known. They may perhaps be classed with reference to three distinct epochs, as the very ancient, the ancient, and those composed from the time of Carolan to that of Jackson and

Stirling; for since the death of the latter composer, the production of new melodies in Ireland has wholly ceased.

The extreme antiquity of the first class, consisting of *caoinans* or dirges, and of airs to which Ossianic and other very old poems are sung, is proved as well by the originality of their structure, (being neither perfect recitative nor perfect melody, but a peculiar combination of both,) as by the fact of their being still sung with the same words in different parts of the country, these words in many instances corresponding exactly with poems of an extremely early date, preserved in ancient manuscripts. Thus, the Lamentation of Deirdre over the Sons of Usnach, is still sung in various parts of the country,[a] to words corresponding with those of the old national romance of the death of the Sons of Usnach, as preserved in Connaught, and printed in the Transactions of the Iberno-Celtic Society. This romance is accounted one of the oldest of the traditionary stories of the country, ranking in antiquity with that of the Children of Lir, and bearing every mark of having been composed in Pagan times. Again, the *goll* to the great *caoinan* or dirge, another air, which probably has its origin in the same ages, answers exactly to the rythm and cadence of those words which, the Editor is informed by Mr. Petrie, are recorded in the Book of Ballymote, to have been sung by a choir of mysterious beings over the grave of a King of Ossory in the tenth century, and of which some stanzas associated with the tune are still remembered in the county of Londonderry. In like manner, the Ossianic airs have been noted down from persons, singing very old fragments of this class of poems, both in Scotland and in Ireland. Of these, perhaps, the most interesting is the air entitled "Erragon More," being that to which the Antrim Glen's people sing the Ossianic fragment published from another source by Dr. Young, in the first volume of the Transactions of the Royal Irish Academy.

Satisfied, on these grounds, that the airs of the first class are all of very great antiquity, the Editor has taken pains to examine and analyze their structure ; and the result has been, that in them he can trace a characteristic style which prevails more or less throughout all genuine Irish music, and constitutes the true test by which to distinguish our native melodies from those of all other countries. It is by the prevalence of this peculiar character, that we become satisfied both of the antiquity and genuineness of a numerous class of airs, where the names of the composers, as is frequently the case, happen to be unknown. And here it may be necessary to observe, that, judging from the words now sung to many of these antique

[a] The Editor had his set from a native of Murlogh, near Ballycastle, in the County Antrim. It is worthy of remark, that the same air and words are sung by natives of Scotland. A blind woman from Cantyre gave the identical notes in singing the piece at Belfast about forty years ago.

melodies we might be disposed at first to refer them to comparatively modern times ; but it will be found, that in every instance where this difficulty at first sight presents itself, the genius of the tune and that of the words are altogether dissimilar : the most tenderly plaintive airs being often associated with mean or grotesque verses, which manifestly could never have had their origin in the same tastes or habits that prompted their respective melodies. Such verses have been composed, and are composed to this day, *ad infinitum*, by persons of an ordinary vein of humour through all parts of Ireland ; but neither in Ireland nor elsewhere has any one been found for the last 150 years, and more, able to produce a single strain of music at all comparable to the airs with which these unpolished lyrics are associated. The ablest composers of the present day are disappointed in the attempt to catch their style ; and invariably meet the fate of Geminiani when he endeavoured to compose a second part to "*The Broom of Cowdenknowes.*" Tunes so unapproachably unique, so eminently graceful, so unlike any other music of the nations around us—for, even in Giraldus's time, the Irish music was "not slow and solemn, as in the instruments of Britain, but cheerful, and ending in a sweet concord of sounds"—can never with any shew of reason be attributed to composers living in times of civil discord and daily peril, in penury and comparative barbarism. They bear the impress of better days, when the native nobles of the country cultivated music as a part of education ; and, amid the wreck of our national history, are, perhaps, the most faithful evidences we have still remaining of the mental cultivation and refinement of our ancestors.

Of this class, the one to which the Editor attaches most importance, is the air called "Ballinderry," which, although now sung to English words, in the counties of Down and Antrim, bears unequivocal marks of a very high antiquity, and at the same time possesses the extraordinary peculiarity of a very nearly regular bass called the *Cronan*, running concurrent with the melody through the entire composition. The Editor, therefore, conceives himself well justified in drawing the conclusion, that those expressions of Cambrensis and others, which intimate, as plainly as words can, that the Irish of their time had a knowledge of counterpoint, or music in consonance, cannot by any ingenuity or dogmatism, whether of Mr. Moore or of Mr. Pinkerton, be drawn from their palpable acceptation as the simple record of the *fact*, a fact honourable to Irish music, and the establishment of which gives the Editor a satisfaction that antiquaries might envy. When the musical inquirer has studied this piece, and the highly curious Lesson and Prelude of the sixteenth century, by Scott, he will be better able to judge of the degree of importance which should be attached to the assertion "That it is certain that our finest airs are *modern* ;" and that, "perhaps, we may look no farther than the *last disgraceful century* for the origin of most of those wild and melancholy strains which were at once the offspring and solace of our grief."[a]

The remainder of the airs which might be reckoned in the second class would be found to consist of numerous pieces not before published, for the most part by unknown hands; but embracing specimens of the composition of O'Cahan, Scott, Daly, and Conallon, all men famous in their day, and still remembered with veneration by the native musicians. Two ancient airs, with variations in the old Irish style, arranged by Lyons, harper to Lord Antrim, about the beginning of the last century, will be found among the most interesting of these.

The airs which may be referred to the third class are nearly all of ascertained origin, and, as has been mentioned, contain nothing of a date much prior to the time of Carolan. A more ornamental and less nervous style is here perceptible. The taste for Italian music, introduced by Geminiani and Corelli, seems about this time to have largely infected the works of Irish composers, especially those of Carolan. The public has been much too apt to regulate its estimate of Irish music by the standard of Carolan's performances. Without detracting from the eminent merits of this composer, it may, however, be safely said that there are many airs of the collection greatly superior to his. Movements with wildly luxuriant basses were those to which his genius chiefly inclined, and in these, indeed, it revelled with surprising gracefulness and freedom. But to the "deep sorrows" of the Irish lyre he rarely aspired. That inimitable vein of tender expression which winds through the very old music of Ireland, in every mood, major or minor, is too often sought for in vain in those compositions, the sweetest of which seldom rise above the tender solicitations of love. His pieces have none of those "tinklings of the small strings, sporting with freedom under the deep notes of the bass," so characteristic of the style of performance among the old harpers, and which may almost be said to snatch a grace beyond the reach of art. The air "Bridget Cruise," esteemed to be the earliest effort of his youth, and inspired by the ardour of a youthful passion, is almost his only attempt at the old style. His imitation of Corelli in other pieces is very apparent, particularly in the responses between the treble and bass, in his "Concerto," "Madam Bermingham," "Lady Blaney," "Colonel O'Hara," "Mrs. Crofton," and "Madam Cole."

Prefixed to the collection, is a dissertation on the antiquity of our national music, containing the result of the Editor's inquiries into its characteristic structure, and accompanied

[a] Prefatory Letter, 3rd vol. Irish Melodies.

by a practical exposition of the modes of performance known to our ancestors. This inquiry is further carried out by an investigation into the antiquity of the Irish Harp and Bagpipe, communicated by the Editor's learned friend, Samuel Ferguson, Esq., M. R. I. A., and comprising a memoir by George Petrie, Esq., M. R. I. A., of that ancient and beautiful instrument usually known as the harp of "King Brian Boru."

While forming these collections the Editor had an opportunity, never, perhaps, enjoyed by any other musical compiler, of rendering himself thoroughly acquainted with the genius and habits of the old native people of the country. His plan would have been imperfect had he had not resorted to the artless modulations of the aged heads of families, and of females taught by their parents to sing to children on the breast, or at the milking of the cow ; an occupation in which the native Irish took particular delight. In these excursions, especially in the remote parts of Tyrone and Derry in Ulster, and of Sligo and Mayo in Connaught, he has had the satisfaction of procuring old music and experiencing ancient hospitality, at the same time, among people of manners so primitive and sincere, as could leave no doubt on any mind of the perfect genuineness of every thing about them. Had he gained nothing else on these occasions but a knowledge of the worth and warmheartedness of his poor countrymen, a knowledge so little sought after by those who might turn it to the best account, he would have been well repaid for all his toil. But this acquaintance with the humours and dispositions of the people, has, he conceives, enabled him to preserve with a fidelity unattainable by any stranger, however sincere and honest in his notation, the pure, racy, old style and sentiment of every bar and note in his collection. While engaged in these searches, he also became acquainted with many curious particulars relating both to the tunes themselves, and to the lives and habits of the later harpers. These notices, combined with original matter, either procured by the Editor's own observation, or from original sources among the cotemporaries of his early years, are also annexed. He has likewise, in connexion with the lives of the harpers, given some account of the various efforts made from time to time for the revival of the national music of Ireland, exertions which, although they have failed in their great object, were at least instrumental in securing a comfortable asylum for the last of our native minstrels. Being now uncertain whether he may again have an opportunity of entering the field in defence of his country's just musical pretensions, the Editor has also taken this occasion to animadvert with some freedom on certain plagiarisms of Irish music, plagiarisms which have been from day to day repeated without shame and without rebuke.

Considering the great degree of interest attaching to everything connected with the ancient state of Ireland, and conscious of having thus done his best for a subject not only intimately associated with the history and antiquities of the country, but very agreeable and popular in its own nature, the Editor does, he confesses, entertain a hope that the collection will be received with approbation by the lovers of music and the learned on both sides of the Channel. Should this be the case, he proposes to re-arrange and republish, with notices of the airs, similar to those of the present publication, the two volumes above spoken of. For it would be his ambition, as he was the first to give to the world a regularly arranged selection of our national airs, to terminate his labours by leaving behind him a complete, uniform, and, he trusts, very nearly perfect, collection of native Irish music.

ANCIENT MUSIC OF IRELAND.

CHAPTER I.

OF THE CHARACTERISTICS OF IRISH MELODY.

Irish Melodies may be distinguished, as to their minor characteristics, into two classes, those, namely, which are marked by the omission of the fourth and seventh tones of the diatonic scale, or one of them, such as the air of

And those which, although also quite Irish in their structure, are not so characterized, such as the air of

These subordinate distinctions have been often observed, and arguments derogatory to the antiquity of our best music have been very confidently advanced on their authority; for, it has been urged, the only assignable characteristics of genuine Irish melody being those of omission, we must refer the more elaborate class of airs in which such omissions do not occur, to a less national and more modernized school. Having thus assumed that the airs of the first class are the more ancient, and seeing that such performances are more likely to have drawn their origin from a defective instrument, such as the ancient bagpipe, which was incapable of properly producing either of the omitted tones, these reasoners go on to argue in like manner against the antiquity of the Irish harp: for, say they, if the tunes proper to the pipes or to the six-stringed cruit, be older than those which can only be performed on the harp, we must of necessity conclude that the latter instrument is of proportionably more recent introduction here than the former; and thus both the antiquity of our national instrument, and the genuineness of those airs of which it is so peculiarly worthy, are impugned on common grounds.

These conclusions, gratifying as they may be to nations which have no genuine music of their own to boast of, spring from the fundamental error of considering the omission of the tones of the fourth and seventh to be the grand characteristic which really marks all Irish melody, and which truly distinguishes it from that of other countries. Now, the fact is, that these omissions are not the true tokens of our national and ancient music. They occur in some airs, not in all; and yet all are equally characteristic, all equally Irish, and some, marked by the uniform presence of both these tones, are the most Irish, and the most ancient of all. The feature which in truth distinguishes all Irish melody, whether proper to the defective bagpipe, or suited to the perfect harp, is not the negative *omission*, but the positive and emphatic *presence* of a particular tone; and this tone is that of the Submediant, or Major Sixth; in other words, the tone of E in the scale of G. This it is that stamps the true Scotic character (for we Irish are the original Scoti) on every bar of the air in which it occurs, so that the moment this tone is heard, we exclaim, "that is an Irish melody."

If ever the symmetrical relation of musical vibrations should be determined,—and a great step has already been taken in that direction by the inventor of the Kaleidophone,[a]—we may expect to find some exact mode of accounting physically for this phenomenon; but in the present state of musical science, we are unable to do more than assert the fact, that peculiar and deeply delightful sensations attend the intonation of this chord when struck in a sequence of musical sounds, sensations which thrill every ear, and may truly be said to touch the "leading sinews" of the Irish heart.

There are many hundred genuine Irish airs, some of them defective in the fourth and seventh, some supplying the place of the latter by a flat seventh, and others, again, perfect

[a] In this ingenious instrument upright wires, fixed at the lower extremity, being made to vibrate, a silvered bead on the top of each catches the light, and exhibits the path of the vibrations. These paths are beautifully symmetrical, forming figures of great intricacy and variety.

Could not these wires be made to vibrate in musical tones, according to a scale, so as to exhibit the physical relations of sounds in musical succession?

in all their diatonic intervals; yet let even an indifferent ear catch the strain of any one of them, whether performed by the best orchestra or by the meanest street musician, and it will at once feel thrilled by this searching tone of the emphatic Major Sixth, and in that touching and tingling sensation will recognize the proper voice of the Land of Song.

The Irish school of music is, therefore, not a school of omissions and affected deficiencies, drawing its examples from the tones of a barbarian bagpipe, but a school of sweet and perfect harmony, proper to a harp of many strings, and suited in its intricate and florid character to cultivated ears and civilized assemblies.

We now proceed to illustrate the peculiar use and application of their grand characteristic in two of our native airs, the first defective in the fourth and seventh, the second perfect in all its intervals, yet both equally marked by the recurrence of the emphatic Major Sixth, which in the subjoined examples is indicated by an asterisk.

Such, in the Editor's opinion, is the grand characteristic of Irish melody, a characteristic which pervades alike the defective class of song and pipe tunes, such as the first in the above examples, and the perfect harp lessons represented by the latter.

Independently of these particular features, Irish melody has also its own peculiarity of structure and arrangement, but this is more observable in the very old class of airs. These airs are for the most part in a major key, and in triple time ; the modulation of the first part of the melody may be said to consist of the common cadence ; the second part is generally an octave higher than the first ; it begins with the chord of the Tonic, and proceeds to the Dominant with its major concord ; it then returns to the Tonic, from which it progresses to the tone of the Submediant with the major harmony of the Subdominant, or to the Submediant with its minor concord ; but the harmony of this peculiar note is most frequently accompanied by the major concord of the Subdominant ; the conclusion of the air is generally a repetition of the first part of the tune, with a little variation. This constitutes the structure and modulation of three-fourths of our song and harp airs, and the main features of such an arrangement, namely, their being principally in a major key, and in triple time, the rise of an octave in the second part, and the repetition of the first part at the conclusion, with the modulation as above, are markedly observable in the composition of our most ancient melodies. Various harmonies, dependent on the taste or science of the musician, might be adapted to those old airs, but it is presumed the above will be found to be the most correct and suitable. The most ancient, it may be observed, will be found more easily harmonized than those of a more modern date ; a certain indication of the greater purity of their structure.

It will be observed, that the tones of the Dominant and Subdominant, with their corresponding concords and modulation above described, agree in a remarkable manner with the *diapente* and *diatesseron* of Cambrensis. Would it, then, be too much to surmise that that writer was, himself, acquainted with these peculiarities in the structure of Irish melody, which have so long eluded the search of modern musicians, and that this famous account of Irish music in the twelfth century which he has given us, is actually a scientific description of the modulation of a genuine Irish tune, as preserved to the present day ?

Irish song music being thus carefully adjusted to one standard of arrangement, a conjecture may be hazarded as to the character of the original melody on which the whole school has been founded.

"*The Young Man's Dream,*" and the air of "*The Green Woods of Truigha,*" might be suggested as answering more nearly to the Editor's conception of such a standard than any others with which he is acquainted. The latter melody is of great antiquity, as is proved both by its structure, and by the fact of its being known by so many different names in different parts of the country. Thus, it is known in Ulster as "*The Green Woods of Truigha,*" in Leinster as "*Edmund of the Hill,*" in Connaught as "*Colonel O'Gara,*" and in Munster as "*More No Beg,*" with a variety of other aliases.

"Aisling an Oigfir." "*The Young Man's Dream.*"

Distinctly and lively.

"Chuillte Glassan Truigha." "*The Green Woods of Truigha.*"

Moderately quick.

A few of these airs are in common time, and composed of four parts or strains each, the modulation and harmony as already described, such as the popular air of "Molly Astore," taken from the very ancient air of "Molly Bheag O."[a]

"Molli Astore." "*Mary, my Treasure.*"

Moderately quick.

[a] We find an able critique on this class of airs in the *Dublin Examiner* for August, 1816. "For the most part, they are formed of four strains of equal length. The first, soft, pathetic, and subdued : the second ascends in the scale, and becomes bold, energetic, and impassioned : the third, a repetition of the second, is sometimes a little varied and more florid, and leads often, by a graceful or melancholy passage, to the fourth, which is always a repetition of the first."

These specimens may be considered as the skeletons of most of our song airs. But it would be impossible to assign any similar model for harp tunes, which are infinitely varied and artful in their arrangement, strongly resembling the vigorous productions of the modern German school, but which, from the predominance of the Major Sixth, or Submediant with its suitable harmony, still sound equally Irish with the most characteristic of the defective class.[a]

From these considerations, grounded on the structure of the airs themselves, we may conclude that the comparative antiquity of the two classes of airs (both being now proved equally genuine) may be determined by the comparative antiquity of the instruments to which they are adapted; and if, as shall presently appear, the harp and bagpipe be both found to be of immemorial use in Ireland, we shall be entitled to claim for the ancient Irish school of music the credit of a very elaborate, artful, and refined style of composition.

Before proceeding, however, to substantiate the claims of our best music to this high antiquity, by inquiring into the early use of these instruments among the Irish, it will be proper to notice the peculiar method of playing practised by the old Irish harpers, whose musical vocabulary, it will be seen, involves another very cogent argument for the great antiquity of their art.

CHAPTER II.

OF THE METHOD OF PLAYING, AND MUSICAL VOCABULARY OF THE OLD IRISH HARPERS.

The world has been too apt to judge of our music as of a peculiarly plaintive character, partaking of our national feelings in a political point of view, and melancholy in proportion to the prospects of its composers. Nothing can be more erroneous than this idea. When the meeting of the harpers took place at Belfast, in 1792, the Editor, being selected to note down the tunes, was surprised to find that all the melodies played by the harpers were performed with a much greater degree of quickness than he had till then been accustomed to. The harpers made those airs assume quite a new character, spirited, lively, and energetic, certainly according much more with the national disposition, than the languid and tedious manner in which they were, and too often still are, played among fashionable public

[a] It does not appear that the later Irish harpers were acquainted with the terms *major* or *minor*, or their application; but they were well apprised of the importance of the harmony attached to the tone of E, and its minor conchord, as appears from the frequent use they made of it, this tone ranking in their estimation next to the key note or tonic.

performers, in whose efforts at realizing a false conception of sentiment, the melody is very often so attenuated as to be all but lost.[a]

In playing, the harpers used a great degree of execution, performing such a variety of difficult and novel shakes, and exhibiting such a precision in *staccato* and *legato*, as astonished and delighted all the musicians present. Struck with the extraordinary degree of art exhibited in these niceties of their performance, the Editor carefully noted down examples of each, taking pains, at the same time, to learn as many as possible of the technical terms by which such points of execution are described in the Irish language. Having subsequently increased his stock of musical terms and examples, from several sources, he is now enabled to present a pretty full digest of ancient Irish musical science; for that these elegancies of execution are of high antiquity, is apparent from the following considerations.

The Irish harpers, when assembled in Belfast, in 1792, uniformly made use of technical terms designating the several notes of the instrument and their various combinations, shakes, moods, &c., which, although admirably characteristic and descriptive in themselves, are altogether unlike the language of modern musicians, a language which is well known to have been invented, at a comparatively recent period, by the continental nations. Had the Irish derived their knowledge of music from nations making use of the continental vocabulary, they would have received the terms of art employed by these nations into their own language, either by adopting them absolutely, or by translating them into corresponding Irish phrases. But the contrary is invariably found to be the case. Thus, that combination of notes termed a *shake* by the modern musicians, is by the Irish denominated barluiṫ, signifying "activity of the fingers; *a beat*, again, is termed barluiṫ beal anarde, or, "activity of finger ends striking upwards;" and a run of execution, Sruiṫ-mor, or, "the great stream." In like manner the principal *times* have their independent and native designations, as Cuigraṫ, "dirge time;" Cuṁadṫ, "lamentation time;" Cruaiḋcleraḋ, "heroic time; Phurt, "lesson time," corresponding to the modern terms *Adagio*, *Larghetto*, *Andante*, and *Allegro*. So also of the chords, moods, keys, &c.

But what even more strongly proves the fact that these modes of execution, with their proper designations, were invented by the Irish people themselves, independently of any assistance from the modern school, is, that many of the peculiarities of performance and terms of art preserved by the Irish are found to have no prototypes or parallels whatever in the continental practice or vocabulary. There is nothing in existence resembling them, if we except the musical method and vocabulary of the Welsh, who are admitted to have derived much of their skill in music from Irish instructors.

The following collection of these native terms of art was procured from the most distinguished of the harpers who met at Belfast, in the year 1792. Their vast importance

[a] Whatever reputation the Editor has acquired, as a performer of Irish music, he owes to no superiority over others, save that of playing the melodies in proper time, and as an humble imitator of the animated manner peculiar to our old harpers.

in establishing the antiquity of the country's music was first pointed out to the Editor by Doctor James M'Donnell, of that town, who zealously assisted in forming the collection. The harpers whose authority was chiefly relied on were Hempson, O'Neill, Higgins, Fanning, and Black, some account of each of whom will be found in another part of this work. Although educated by different masters, (through the medium of the Irish language alone,) and in different parts of the country, they exhibited a perfect agreement in all their statements, referring to the old traditions of the art as their only authority, and professing themselves quite at a loss to explain their method of playing by any other terms.

A general vocabulary of Irish musical terms, so far as the Editor has been able to collect them from the remaining authorities, will be found annexed. Both collections are, no doubt, imperfect; for the sources of written information on the subject are equally difficult of access and of interpretation, and with respect to the traditionary statements of the harpers themselves, it must be recollected that Irish music has been on the wane, at least since the reign of Elizabeth, and that, as the Belfast meeting was in fact the expiring flicker of the lamp that once shed its lustre over Christendom, the Editor cannot be expected to have done more than catch some straggling rays, which are still, however, brilliant enough to show how illustrious an instrument the Irish harp has been in former ages.

THE DIFFERENT KINDS OF IRISH HARPS.

NAMES IN IRISH CHARACTERS.	NAMES IN ENGLISH CHARACTERS.	EXPLANATION.
Clairseach, ...	Clarsech, ...	The common harp.
Cinnard cruit, . . .	Cinnard-Cruit, . .	The high-headed harp.
Crom-chuit, ...	Crom-Cruit, . .	The down-bending harp.
Ceirnin, ...	Ceirnin, ...	Supposed to be the portable harp, used by the priests and religious people.[a]
Craiftin-chruit, . .	Craiftin Cruit, . .	Craftin's harp, (a man noted in Irish legends.)
Lub, ...	Lub, ...	A poetical name of the harp.
THE PARTS OF THE HARP.		
Com, ...	Com, ...	Its waist or belly.
Cor, ...	Cor, ...	The pin board.
Cru na d-tead, . . .	Crunatted, . . .	Shoe of the strings, the piece of brass on the sound board, through which the strings pass.
An foirshnadhm, . .	Aufhoirshnadhaim,	The wooden pegs to which the strings are fastened.
Lamhcrann, ...	Lamchrann, . . .	The front pillar.

[a] "A harp was found about the year 1805, in the bog of Drawling, near Limerick, twelve feet under the surface, made of red sallow, and had on it when found three brass strings. It was about thirty inches long and ten broad."—(Letter from Mr. Corbett, 1809.)

THE STRINGS OF THE HARP.

NAMES IN IRISH CHARACTERS.	NAMES IN ENGLISH CHARACTERS.	TRANSLATION.	MUSICAL EXAMPLES.
caomhluighe,[a]	Caomhluighe, ...	Lying together, .	 G G
guaille caomhluidhe, . . .	Gilly Caomluighe, . . .	Servant to the sisters,	 A
an dara tead os cionn caomluidhe, ...	An dara tead os cionn Caomluighe, ...	Second string over the sisters, . .	 B
an treas tead os cionn caomhluidhe, ...	An treas tead os cionn Caomluighe, ...	Third string over the sisters, . .	 C'
tead na feitheolach,[b] . .	Tead na feithe-o-lach, . .	String of the leading sinews, . .	 D
guaille tead na feitheolach, ...	Gilly Tead na feithe-o-lach,	Servant to the leading sinews, . .	 E
tead a' leithghleas,[c] . . .	Tead a leith glass, . . .	String of the half note, ...	 F
dofhreagrach caomhluidhe,[d]	Dofhregrach Caomluighe,	Answering, . . .	 G

[a] Called by the harpers "The Sisters," were two strings in unison, which were the first tuned to the proper pitch; they answered to tenor G, fourth string on the violin, and nearly divided the instrument into bass and treble.

[b] Called by the old harpers "The String of Melody," was tuned next to the sisters, being a fifth above them.

[c] Next the octave to the sisters.

[d] Octave above the sisters, was next tuned.

THE STRINGS OF THE HARP.—*Continued.*

NAMES IN IRISH CHARACTERS.	NAMES IN ENGLISH CHARACTERS.	TRANSLATION.	MUSICAL EXAMPLES.
Freagrach tead na feitheolach,[a]	Freagrach tead na feithe-o-lach, ...	Response to leading sinews, . . .	D
Cronan,[b]	Cronan, ...	Drone bass, . . .	G
Tead leagaidh,[c]	Tead leaguidh, ...	Falling string, . .	F
Tead leagtha,[d]	Tead leacthea, ...	The string fallen, .	E
Cronan iochtar-chanus,[e] .	Cronan ioch-dar-chanus, .	Lowest note, . .	C C
Uachtar-chanus,[f]	Uach-dar-chanus, . . .	Highest note, . .	D
Dofhreagrach,[g]	Do Fregrach, ...	Answering, . . .	
Fhreagrach,[h]	Fregrach, ...	Response, . . .	

[a] Being octave below the string of melody.
[b] Octave below the sisters.
[c] Being F natural raised from E natural, a semitone, to answer the melody as occasion required.
[d] The natural tone of the string.
[e] Double C in the bass, five notes below the cronan.
[f] D in alt, the highest note on the Irish harp.
[g] Applied to all the octaves in the treble.
[h] Applied to all the octaves in the bass, except the cronan.

SCALE OF THE IRISH HARP OF THIRTY STRINGS, TUNED IN THE NATURAL KEY, TERMED,

"Leath Gleas," *or half note.*

METHOD OF TUNING USED BY THE OLD HARPERS.

Tuned for high bass key.

Tuned in octaves to the top. Tuned in octaves to the bottom.‡

C sharp,§ 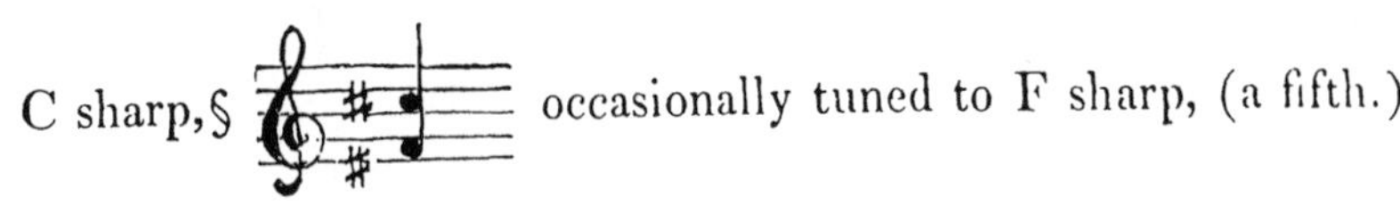 occasionally tuned to F sharp, (a fifth.)

* The Irish harp had no string for F sharp, between E and G in the bass, probably because it had no concord in their scale for that tone, either major or minor; but this E in the bass, called "Teadlecthae," or *fallen* string, in the natural key termed "Leath Glass," being altered to F natural, a semitone higher when the melody required it, and the sharp F's, through the instrument being previously lowered a semitone, the key was then called "Teadleaguidhe," the *falling* string, or high bass key.

† This is the number of strings indicated by the string holes on the sound board of the ancient Irish harp, now in Trinity College, Dublin, erroneously called "Brian Boiromhe's Harp," and was the usual number of strings found on all the harps at the Belfast meeting, in 1792.

‡ It will be observed by the musical critic, that only two major keys, viz., G one sharp, and C natural, were perfect in their diatonic intervals on the Irish harp; but the harpers also made use of two ancient diatonic minor keys, (neither of them perfect according to the modern scale,) viz., E one sharp, and A natural. They sometimes made use of D natural minor, which was still more imperfect, though some of their airs were performed in that key, and were thought extremely agreeable by many persons.

§ The harpers said that this single note, C sharp, was sometimes made use of, but the Editor seldom met with an instance of it.

GRACES PERFORMED BY THE TREBLE OR LEFT HAND.[a]

NAMES IN IRISH CHARACTERS.	NAMES IN ENGLISH CHARACTERS.	TRANSLATION.	MUSICAL EXAMPLES.
Brisidh,[b]	Brisidh, ...	A break, ...	 &c.
Leagadh anuas,[c] . .	Leagadh anuas, . .	A falling, . . .	 &c.
Leith leagadh,[d] . . .	Leath leaguidh, . .	A half falling, . .	 &c.
Sruth mor, ...	Sruith-mor, . . .	A great stream, ascending,[e] . .	
		Or descending,[f] .	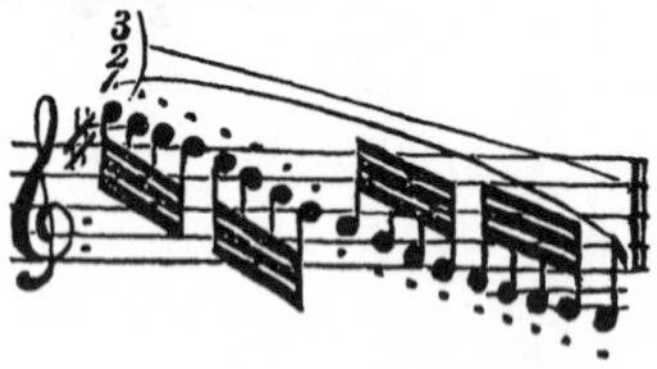
Sruth beag,[g]	Sruith-beg, . . .	Little stream, . .	 &c.....

[a] The Irish harpers played the treble with the left hand, and the bass with the right. The Welsh performed on their national harp in the same manner.

[b] Performed by the thumb and first finger; the string struck by the thumb is stopped by it, and first finger string left sounding.

[c] By first finger and thumb; thumb stops the string sounded by first finger, and thumb string left sounding.

[d] By second and third finger; string struck by second, stopped by first, and string struck by third, stopped by second finger.

[e] First, second, and third fingers of left hand slid along the strings, which were either stopped or allowed to sound, as the harper pleased; in general executed in the most rapid manner.

[f] Fingered in same manner as last by right hand, performed as above.

[g] By thumb, first, second, and third fingers of the left hand.

Graces performed by the Treble or Left Hand.—*Continued.*

NAMES IN IRISH CHARACTERS.	NAMES IN ENGLISH CHARACTERS.	TRANSLATION.	MUSICAL EXAMPLES.
bualadh suas no suaserigh,[a] . . .	Bualladh suas no suaserigh, .	Succession of triplets, ...	
SHAKES, ETC.			
barrluth,[b]	Barlluith, . . .	Activity of fingers,	
barrluth beal an-airde,[c]	Barlluith-beal-an-airdhe, . . .	Activity of finger ends, striking upwards, . . .	
casluth,[d]	Casluith, ...	Returning actively,	
barrluth fosgailte,[e]	Barluith fosgalta, .	Activity of finger tops, ...	
cul-aithris,[f]	Cul-aithris, . . .	Half shake, . . .	
tribhuilleach no creathadh coimh-mhear,[g]	Tribuilleach or creathadh coimh-mhear, . . .	Triple shake, . .	

[a] By third, second, and first fingers, ascending one string each time.

[b] A continued shake, by second, first, and third fingers, alternately. The harpers did not finish the shake with a turn, as in the mode adopted at present.

[c] By second, first, and third fingers; the string struck by third, briskly stopped by second, first string still sounding.

[d] By third, first, and second fingers; the strings stopped instantaneously by each finger when played.

[e] By second, first, and third fingers; second finger string stopped by first; first finger string still sounding.

[f] By first finger and thumb.

[g] By second, first, and third fingers, three times in succession.

GRACES PERFORMED BY THE TREBLE OR LEFT HAND.—*Continued.*

NAMES IN IRISH CHARACTERS.	NAMES IN ENGLISH CHARACTERS.	TRANSLATION.	MUSICAL EXAMPLES.
crotach aon mear,[a]	Crothachaon mhear,	Shaking, ...	

DOUBLE NOTES, CHORDS, ETC.

FOR THE LEFT HAND.

NAMES IN IRISH CHARACTERS.	NAMES IN ENGLISH CHARACTERS.	TRANSLATION.	MUSICAL EXAMPLES.
bolsgan,[b]	Bulsgan, ...	Swelling out, . .	
glas,[c]	Glass, ...	A joining, . . .	
FOR THE RIGHT HAND.			
glas,[d]	Glass, ...	A joining, . . .	
ladhar,[e]	Laghar, ...	Spread hand, . .	
ladhar lair,[f]	Lagharlair, . . .	Middle of hand, .	

[a] By first finger, back and forwards, on the same string.

[b] By first and second fingers, a third.

[c] By first and third fingers, a fourth.

[d] By thumb and third finger, an octave.

[e] With forked fingers, first and third fingers, an octave.

[f] By first and second fingers, a third.

Double Notes, Chords, etc.—*Continued.*

NAMES IN IRISH CHARACTERS.	NAMES IN ENGLISH CHARACTERS.	TRANSLATION.	MUSICAL EXAMPLES.
glasluth,[a]	Glasluith, . . .	Quick locking, . .	
ceann an chroibh,[b]	Cennanchruich, .	Extremity of hand,	
taobhcrobh,[c]	Taobhcrobh, . .	Side hand, . . .	
lanchrobh,[d]	Lanchrobh, . . .	Full hand, . . .	
malairt phonch,[e] .	Malart Phonch, .	To reverse the hand,	

It is worthy of remark, that the harpers struck the upper note of these chords first, instead of beginning with the lowest tone, as the moderns do in their Arpeggios. All these graces, shakes, double notes, chords, &c., had a different sound and expression, according to the method adopted in fingering, and stopping the vibration of the strings.

[a] By thumb, first and third fingers; a chord of a third, with an octave.

[b] By first, second, and third fingers; a chord of three notes.

[c] By thumb, second, and third fingers; a chord of three notes.

[d] By thumb, first, second, and third fingers; a chord of four notes.

[e] Or crossing the hands, the right hand taking the place of the left.

THE TIME.

NAMES IN IRISH CHARACTERS.	NAMES IN ENGLISH CHARACTERS.	TRANSLATION.	EXPLANATION.
trebhuinneach, . .	Trebhuinneach, .	Trebly rapid. . .	Irish jig time, used in the old dancing airs, &c., which were performed with great vivacity and vigour.
cuigrath, ...	Cuigrath, ...	Dirge time. . . .	Lamentations for particular families, with words.
cruaidhchleasach,	Crudhchlesach, . .	Bold, heroic. . .	Marching time, also the time of the ancient melodies in general.
cumhadh, ...	Cumhadth, . . .	Lamentation. . .	Time of the music composed in compliment to the deceased patrons of the harpers, without words, but by no means slowly played.
port, ...	Phurt, ...	Time of the lessons.	"Phurt" frequently consisted of two parts, first, *Na phurt*, introductory, and *Malart Phonck*, changing the position of the hands, the right hand playing the treble and the left the bass.

THE MOODS.

NAMES IN IRISH CHARACTERS.	NAMES IN ENGLISH CHARACTERS.	TRANSLATION.	EXPLANATION.
adbhan trireach, .	Alhbhan-trirech, .	The three moods, .	Or species of music.
geantraighe, . . .	Geanttraidheacht, .	Love.	Music of a graceful and expressive order.
golltraighe, ...	Gollttraidheacht, .	Exciting sorrow. .	Melancholy music.
suantraighe, . . .	Suanttraidheacht, .	Soothing. . . .	Sleepy, composing strains.
luinneach, ...	Luinneach, . . .	Merry, jovial music.	Supposed to apply to the Luinigs of the Highlands of Scotland.

THE KEYS.

NAMES IN IRISH CHARACTERS.	NAMES IN ENGLISH CHARACTERS.	TRANSLATION.	EXPLANATION.
leithghleas, ...	Leath glass, . .	Half note. . . .	The leading, or next note to the "response," to the "sisters," forming the proper key of the harp, being G natural, one sharp.
fuigheall mor, . .	Fuigheall-mor, . .	Great sound. . .	Formed by raising C natural (a semitone higher) to C sharp. Seldom used.
fuigheall beag, . .	Fuigheall-beg, . .	Lesser sound. . .	Supposed to be high bass, or flat key.
aon-fuigheall, . .	Uan fuigheall, . .	Single sound. . .	One sharp, another name for the key of G.

As a further evidence of the richness, as well as independence of the Irish language, in terms of musical art in general, the following Vocabulary has been compiled from the various dictionaries of the language and other sources, and is now submitted, as evidencing, with the preceding digest, a wonderful mass of musical acquirements in an apparently self-taught community.

A GENERAL VOCABULARY

OF

ANCIENT IRISH MUSICAL TERMS,

ARRANGED FROM THE VARIOUS DICTIONARIES OF THE LANGUAGE,

AND OTHER SOURCES.

Those terms marked thus (*) are taken from the twenty-four measures of Welch music. Those marked thus (†) from the information of Arthur O'Neill, &c. The remainder from the various dictionaries of the language, Lluyd, &c., from the earliest to the most modern.

A.	A.	
Aḋḃan trireaċ,	Adbhan trireach,	A species of music which is divided into three parts, viz., *Gean troighe*, exhilarating ; *Goll troighe*, affecting ; and *Suan troighe*, soothing.
Aiḋse,	Aidhbhsi,	A species of music formerly in use, an old song or cronan.
Aine,	Aine,	Music, harmony.
Airaṫlaniffad,	Airathlaniffad,*	A full repetition.
Airfideaċ,	Airfideach, or Dafideadh,	Music, a musician, harmony.
Allṁaraċ,	Allmharach,*	Foreign strain.
Aṁan, or Aṁar,	Amhan,	Music.
Aṁrán,	Amhran,	A song.
Aṁraḋ,	Amiradh,	An elegy for the dead.
Anḟoirṡnaḋaim,	Anfhoirshnadhaim,†	The pin board, or wooden pegs, to which the strings are fastened.
Aos ceóil,	Aois ceiol,	Musicians.

b.	B.	
barluiṫ,	Barluith,	Activity of fingers, a continued shake.
barluiṫ buallaḋanáirde,	Barluith bualladhanairde,†	Activity of finger ends striking upwards.
barluiṫ fosgalte,	Barluith fosgalte,†	Activity of finger tops.
basacanas,	Basascanas,	The bass in music.
binn,	Binn,	Melodious, harmonious.
binnas, binni,	Binnas, binni,	Harmony, melody.
biol,	Biol,	A musical instrument.
bhualaḋsuas,	Bhualadhsuas,†	Successive triplets.
braṫanasgol,	Brathanas-gol,*	School strain.
briseaḋ,	Brisidh,†	A break.
bruṫ ḋon druideoig,	Bruth dhon druidoig,*	Soft strain.
boilsgean,	Boilsgean,†	Swelling out.
buan,	Buan,	Harmonious.
buaḃal,	Bualbal,	A cornet or horn.
buallaḋsuas,	Bualladhsuas,†	Ascending.
builsgean,	Builsgan,	A third in music.

C.	C.	
Cairċe,	Cairche,	Music.
Caisneaċd,	Caisneachd,	A tune to which soldiers march.
Callóid,	Calloid,	A funeral elegy.
Calċan,	Calchan,*	A calling strain.
Car,	Car,	A bar, or division in music.
Casluiṫ,	Castluith,†	Returning activity.
Caoineaḋ,	Caoineadh,	Lamentation for the dead.
Ceol,	Ceol,	Melody, music.
Ceirnín,	Ceirnin,	A portable harp.
Cennanċruiḃ,	Cennanchruitbh,†	Extremity of the hand.
Cinnard ċruit,	Cinnard chruit,	High headed harp.
Ciontar,	Cionthar,	Music, melody.
Ciuil,	Ciuil,	Harmony, music.
Clairseaċ,	Clairseach,	A harp.
Clairseoir,	Clairseoir,	A harper.
Clairaiḋe,	Clairaidhe,	A singer, a songster.
Clas blaisceadul, no ceol, no cantaireaċd,	Clas blaisceadul no ceol, no canntaireached,	Melody, harmony.

Com,	Com,†	Waist, or belly of the harp.
Coṁ luiġe,	Combh luighe,†	Equally stretched.
Cor,	Cor,†	Music pin board.
Coronaċ,	Coronach,	An elegy for the dead.
Cor altan,	Cor altan,*	Little joints, music.
Cor coḋlata,	Cor ccodhlata,*	Lulling music.
Cor finn ḟuar,	Cor finn fhuar,*	Music of cool shade.
Cordoṫeaġlaċ,	Cordoteghlach,*	Household music.
Cor ḟineaṁain,	Cor ffineamhain,*	Vintage music.
Cor fairċogaiḋ,	Cor fairchogaidh,*	Warlike music.
Corsiḋ,	Corsidh,*	Pacific music.
Crañ dordain,	Crann dardaion,	A species of bass made by putting the hands to the mouth.
Craṫaċanmer,	Crathachanmer,†	Nimble shake.
Cromcruitean,	Cromcruitan,	Down bending harp.
Cronanioċdarċanus,	Cronaniochdarchanus,	Lowest C in the bass.
Cronán,	Cronan,	The bass in music.
Crotal,	Crotal,	A cymbal.
Cruaḋċosṫaḃiseaċt,	Cruadhchosthaviseacht,	A march.
Cruaḋċosaċ,	Cruadhchosach,	Heroic time.
Cruit,	Cruit,	A harp.
Cruisiġ,	Cruisich,	Cool music.
Cruiteóg,	Cruitoge,	A small violin.
Cruiṫ,	Cruith,	A crowde, or violin.
Cruitire,	Crutaire,	A harper, a musician.
Crunadted,	Crunatted,†	Shoe of the strings, the small piece of brass on the sound board, through which the strings pass.
Cuigeaċ,	Cuigeach,	A fifth.
Cuigeaṫ,	Cuigeath,	A dirge.
Cuis·leannaċ,	Cuisleannach,	A person who plays on a wind instrument.
Cuisleannaġ,	Cuisleanagh,	A pipe, or piper.
Culaiṫris,	Culaithris,†	Repetition, or relish.
Cuṁaċ,	Cumhach,	Sorrowful.
Cuṁaḋ,	Cumhadh,	Lamentation for the dead.
D.	D.	
Doḟreaġreaċ,	Dofhreaghrach,†	Answering, an octave.
Dudóg,	Dudog,	A hunting horn, war trumpet.
Dudaire,	Dudaire,	A trumpet.

E.	E.	
Eardanál,	Eardanal,	A piper, or trumpeter.
Earglan, no Earġalán,	Earglan, or Earghalan,	A piper.
Eardanál fear ḃíos ag fiorḋa nalaiġ,	Eardanal fear bhios ag fiordhanalaigh,	A trumpeter, or piper.
Easnaḋ,	Easnadh,	Music, song, melody.
Easnaḋ ceóil,	Easnedh ceol,	Music.

F.	F.	
Faiteal,	Faiteal,	Music.
Feadán,	Feadan,	A pipe, reed, flute.
Feadóg,	Feadog,	A flute.
Feat,	Feat,	Music, harmony.
Fideog,	Fideog,	A small pipe.
Flám gur guaigin,	Flam gur guaigain,*	Fantasy-strain.
Fleasgaċ,	Fleasgach,	A fiddler.
Fonn,	Fonn,	A tune, a song.
Foġair,	Foghair,	A tone, or ascent.
Foġal,	Foghal,	The whole.
Fore,	Fore,	A song.
Fuaiḋġel mór,	Fuaidhghel-mor,†	Great harmony, or key of D, two sharps.
Fuaiḋġel beag,	Fuaidhghel-beg,†	Little harmony, or key of C.
Fuaim,	Fuaim,	A noise, or sound.

G.	G.	
Gentraġaċ,	Gentraghach,†	Exhilirating.
Glas,	Glas,†	A joining.
Glasluiṫ,	Glasluith,†	Agile, locking.
Galltrumpa,	Goll trompa,	A trumpeter.
Gultraġaċ,	Goltraghach,†	Affecting, or sorrowful.

H.	H.	
Hiṫir,	Hihir,*	Land strain.

I.	I.	
Iḃfasaċ,	Iffasach,*	Wilderness.
Ilḋeanaḋ, no ilġuiḋim,	Ildheanadh, or ilguidhim,	A variation, to vary or alter.

L.	L.	
Laġar,	Laghar,†	Spread hands, with forked fingers.
Laġalair,	Laghalair,†	Middle of the hand.
Lamċran̄,	Lamhchrann,†	Front pillar.
Lancroḃ,	Lanchrobh,†	Full hand.
Laḃiḋ,	Lavidh,	A song.
Leadán,	Leadan,	Musical notes.
Leagaḋ,	Leagudh,†	Half fall.
Leagaḋnuas,	Leaghadhnuas,†	A falling down.
Leiṫglos tar,	Leithglos tar,†	A tune.
Lomna, no téad,	Lomna, or tead,	A string or cord.
Lomnóir,	Lomnoir,	A harper.
Louloingean,	Louloingean,	A pipe.
Lúb,	Lub,†	A poetical name for the harp.
Luinneóg,	Luinneag,	A chorus.
Luin̄eaċ,	Luinneach,	Merry music.
Luṫglas,	Luthglass,†	Natural key.
Luċd seinm,	Luchd seinm,	Musicians.

M.	M.	
Macaduilge,	Macaduilge,*	Plaintive, melancholy strain.
Maġan̄ an aṫar,	Maghaum in thir,*	For the country plains.
Maġan inḃir,	Maghumanmbirr,*	Watery plain, lake-music.
Maġumanṁin,	Magamoinmhin,*	Flowery, plain strain.
Maoḃ,	Maobh,†	Variation.
Marḃran̄,	Marbhrann,	Death song.
Marḃna,	Marbhna,	An elegy for the dead.
Malairt,	Malairt,†	Change of the hand.

O.	O.	
Oċtaiḋeċ,	Ochtaidhech,†	An octave.
Oċiṡlaḃliaċ,	Ochishlabhliach,†	Belonging to an octave.
Oḋ ⁊ oiḋ ceoil,	Odh agus oidh ceol,	Music.
Oirfia,	Oirfia,	Music, melody.
Oirfiḋe, no orṗeam,	Oirfidhe or orpheam,	A harper.
Orán,	Oran,	A song.
Orleaṫ leagaḋ,	Orleath leagadh,†	A falling.

P.	P.	
Peit,	Peit,	A musician.
Peiṫeaḋ airfideaċ ceól,	Peiteadh airfideach ceol,	Harmony, music, song, melody.
Phurt,	Phurt,†	Spirited.
Pib, no piob,	Pib, piob,	A pipe.
Piobṁala,	Piobmhala,	A bagpipe.
Piobaire,	Piobaire,	A piper.
Piobaireaċd,	Piobaireachd,	The pipe music.
Píobṡioñaiċ,	Piobshionach,	A pipe blown with bellows.
Pirpiet,	Pirpiot,	Melody, harmony.
Port,	Port,	A tune.
R.	**R.**	
Rañ,	Rann,	A song.
Riṁṡeiním,	Rimhsheinnim,	To play music.
Rim ceól,	Rimm ceol,	Music.
Riñ,	Rinn,	Music, melody.
Riñárd,	Rinnard,*	High point.
S.	**S.**	
Sallañ,	Sallann,	Singing, harmony.
Seamma,	Seamma,	Of music, musical fear.
Seanma,	Seanma,	Musical, a minstrel.
Seinm,	Seinm,	Singing, also playing on an instrument.
Siansa,	Siansa,	Melody, harmony.
Sruṫ,	Sruith,†	A stream.
Stoc,	Stoc,†	A trumpet or horn.
Suantraiḋeċ,	Suantraighech,	Soothing.
Siuḃal,	Suibhul,	A measure in music between fast and slow.
T.	**T.**	
Taeideaċ,	Taeideach,*	Flowing tide strain.
Taoḃċroḃ,	Taebhchrobh,	Side hand.
Téad,	Tead,†	Sinew, string of a harp, also a harp.
Téadaiḋe,	Teadaidhe,	A harper.
Teañorcanus,	Teannorcanus,	The counter tenor.
Téḋleagṫa,	Tedlectha,	The string fallen.

Tedleagaiḋe,	Tedlegaidhe,†	The falling string.
Ted na féola,	Tednafeola,†	Leading sinews or strings.
Tet,	Tet,	A drum, cymbal.
Tiompán,	Tiompaun,	An elegy.
Tiompan,	Tiompan,	A drum, tymbal or tabor.
Torḋán,	Tordhan,	An elegy.
Toruġán,	Torughan,	Bass in music.
Treisi uillean̄,	Treisi uilenn,*	Force of elbow.
Treḃuin̄eaċ,	Trebhuinnech,†	Prestissimo, trebly rapid.
Tríḃuilleaċ,	Tribhuillech,†	Triple shake.
Triḃuin̄eaċ,	Tribuinneach.	Extremely quick.
Truaġġalmar,	Truaghgholmor,*	High wailing strain.
Truiḋirḃaġac,	Truidhirbhaghac,*	Tenderly affectionate strain.
U.	**U.**	
Uaċdarċanus,	Uachdarchanus,	Highest D in alt.
Uaim,	Uaim,	Notes on the harp, concordance.
Uaim, fuaim,	Uaim, fuaim,†	A sound.
Uan fuaiḋġail,	Uan fuaidhghail,†	A single sound.
Uiḋiḋeaċt,	Uidhidheacht,	Harmony, music.
Uiḋiḋ oḋaḋ, i. e. ceólṁar,	Uidhidh odhadh, i. e. coel-mher,	Musical, harmonious.
Uinaiḋin ceangal, no urs-naiḋm ceangal,	Uinaidhin ceangal,† or urshnaidhm ceangal,	The pin or jack that fastens the wire of the harp.

We now proceed to the next evidence of the antiquity of our best music, which, as has been seen, may be inferred from the date at which the Irish can be proved to have possessed instruments capable of performing it.

Engraved by John Kirkwood Dublin

Ancient Irish Harp in Trinity College Dublin
Right Hand Side View

Published by Hodges & Smith Dublin.

CHAPTER III.

OF THE ANTIQUITY OF THE HARP AND BAGPIPE IN IRELAND.

BY SAMUEL FERGUSON, ESQ., M. R. I. A.

THE Irish harp, as used by the remaining representatives of the old race of harpers, was strung with thirty strings, having a compass from C to D in alt., comprising the tones included between the highest pitch of the female voice and the lowest of the male, being the natural limits within which to construct the scale of an instrument intended to accompany vocal performances. The mode of tuning has already been illustrated. In endeavouring to ascertain the antiquity of this instrument, it is proposed to consider, first, how far the harp in use among the Irish at the period of the Anglo-Norman invasion corresponded with the Irish harp in use at the beginning of the present century, and, secondly, how long before the Anglo-Norman invasion the Irish had possessed the instrument then in use.

From the account given by Cambrensis (in that famous passage respecting the musical skill of the Irish at the time of the Anglo-Norman invasion) of the intricate, rapid, and *crisp* manner of playing practised among our ancestors, especially from his statement as to the simultaneous introduction of high and low notes into their performance, there can be no rational doubt that the instrument which was capable of so highly exciting the delight and admiration of an accomplished ecclesiastic, and one necessarily acquainted with counterpoint, as then cultivated in our churches, must have possessed sufficient compass for the performance of certain pieces of music in consonance. This obvious interpretation of the meaning of the passage, is borne out by a drawing of an Irish harper given by Mr. Planche, in his Costumes of the British People, from an early illuminated MS. of Cambrensis. The performer is here represented as holding the harp on his knee, and playing with both hands. It is difficult to say from the drawing whether he plays the bass with the right or left hand, though, from other illustrations, to be presently adduced, it would appear most probable that the left is raised in the act of striking the chords of the treble, a method of

playing the reverse of that used by modern musicians, who draw their practice from continental teaching, but retained by the old Irish harpers so long as any of that class of performers remained.

It is to be regretted that the number of strings in the drawing before us has not been represented with sufficient care to enable us to judge with certainty of the compass of the instrument; for painters and sculptors generally look more to effect than accuracy, and there is unfortunately no native monument of the harp of any antiquity, except that, perhaps, on the *Fiachal Phadruigh* noticed below, to which this observation does not apply. At the same time, carelessly as the strings are here represented, it seems manifest from the position of the hands that the performer is playing a bass and treble.

The age of the manuscript is not assigned by Mr. Planche, but such illuminations, purporting to be the representations of objects described in the text, are rarely otherwise than cotemporary. Assuming this, however, to be an illumination of the thirteenth century, it brings us to the testimony of Dante, referred to by Galilei the elder, who, writing about the middle of the sixteenth century, thus speaks of the structure and compass of the Irish harp: " *This most ancient instrument* was brought to us from Ireland, as DANTE (born A. D. 1265) says, where they are excellently made and in great numbers, the inhabitants of that island having practised on it *for many and many ages.* * * * The harps which this people use (i. e. in Galilei's time) are considerably larger than ours, and have generally the strings of brass, and a few of steel for the highest notes, as in the *Clavichord.* * * * The number of strings is fifty-four, fifty-six, and in some sixty. * * * I had, a few months since, by the civility of an Irish gentleman, an opportunity of seeing one of their harps, and, after having minutely examined the arrangement of its strings, I found it was the same which, with double the number, was introduced into Italy a few years ago." This would make the number of strings on the last-mentioned harp twenty-nine, for the writer, immediately after this statement, proceeds to give directions for tuning the Italian harp[a] of fifty-eight strings. But when a writer, speaking loosely of numbers, says of one that it is half the amount of another, it cannot be expected that he should note fractional differences, and, therefore, it may be assumed that in speaking of a harp having half as many strings as one which is known to have had fifty-eight, Galilei may have referred not to a harp of twenty-nine, but to one of thirty strings, this number comprehending the compass of four octaves and a tone above referred to. If, then, the common Irish harp in Galilei's time had a compass of thirty strings, and was the same as that which had been introduced into Italy before the time of Dante, we may reasonably conclude that thirty was the number of strings commonly in use at the period of the Anglo-Norman invasion.

A very accurate, though rude, representation of the Irish harp, of the century next after that to which Dante's testimony refers, exists on a curious piece of native workmanship, called the *Fiachal Phadruig*, being the reliquary or portable shrine in which the tooth of St. Patrick (so luminously treated of by various writers in the Irish *Acta, S. S.*) is said to have been formerly preserved. The reliquary is stated by Mr. Petrie, from an Irish inscrip-

[a] Vincent Galilei, Dialogue on Ancient and Modern Music. Florence, 1581. (See the entire passage in Bunting's Ancient Music of Ireland, vol. i. Preliminary Dissertation, pp. 24, 25.)

tion still legible on it, to have been ornamented with the figures, among which the representation in question occurs, by the orders of Thomas de Bramigham, eighth lord of Athenry, about A. D. 1350, and is now in the possession of Sir Valentine Blake, Bart., through whose politeness the subjoined *fac simile* has been obtained. The metal on which the figure is sculptured has been much worn away ; but, from the remaining traces of the harp strings, (which are hardly represented with perfect accuracy on the wood-cut,) they appear to have been originally thirty in number.

Having seen such reason as the foregoing statements and illustrations afford for believing that the Irish harp, prior to the year 1350, possessed in general a compass of thirty strings, or thereabouts, the reader will not fail to perceive the force and conclusiveness of the evidence which is next to be brought forward—not being that of any drawing or description, such as has been above made use of, but the direct testimony of an instrument still in preservation, and capable of speaking for itself, though of at least as great an antiquity as the representation last adduced. The instrument in question is that ancient harp so long known as King Brian Boru's, but which has no legitimate pretensions to that title, as will be seen from the following memoir, kindly communicated by a gentleman who stands *facile princeps* among the Irish antiquaries of the present day. It is now reduced to its proper era, the early part of the fourteenth century ; and here its positive evidence must be allowed to be of the utmost value, coming in as it does in corroboration of the inferences drawn from cotemporaneous but less certain monuments ; for it now appears, on closer examination, that the number of strings on this most interesting relic corresponds exactly with the number above surmised to belong to the Irish harp of the thirteenth and fourteenth centuries, as it also does with the number still in use among our native harpers in our own time.

MEMOIR OF ANCIENT IRISH HARP PRESERVED IN TRINITY COLLEGE.

BY GEORGE PETRIE, ESQ., M. R. I. A.

"The harp preserved in the Museum of Trinity College, Dublin, and popularly known as the harp of Brian Boru, is not only the most ancient instrument of the kind known to exist in Ireland, but is, in all probability, the oldest harp now remaining in Europe. Still, however, it is very far from being of the remote age to which it is popularly supposed to belong; and the legendary story on which this supposition is grounded, and which has been fabricated to raise its antiquity and increase its historical interest, is but a clumsy forgery, which will not bear for a moment the test of critical antiquarian examination. We are told that Donogh, the son and successor of the celebrated Brian Boru, who was killed at the battle of Clontarf in 1014, having murdered his brother Teague, in 1023, was deposed by his nephew, in consequence of which he retired to Rome, carrying with him the crown, harp, and *other* regalia of his father, which he presented to the Pope in order to obtain absolution. 'Adrian IV., surnamed Breakspear, alleged this circumstance as one of the principal titles he claimed to this kingdom, in his bull transferring it to Henry II. These regalia were kept in the Vatican till the Pope sent the harp to Henry VIII., with the title of Defender of the Faith, but kept the crown, which was of massive gold. Henry gave the harp to the first Earl of Clanricarde, in whose family it remained till the beginning of the last century, when it came, by a lady of the De Burg family, into that of Mac Mahon of Clenagh, in the county of Clare, after whose death it passed into the possession of Commissioner Macnamara, of Limerick. In 1782 it was presented to the Right Honourable William [Burton] Conyngham, who deposited it in Trinity College, Dublin.' Such is the story, as framed by the Chevalier O'Gorman, by whom the harp was given to Colonel Burton Conyngham, and, as usual in the fabrication of most romantic legends, the fictitious allegations are so engrafted on real historical facts, the fable is so intermixed with the truth, that few readers would think of doubting one more than the other, or, even if they should doubt, would have the power of distinguishing between them. Thus, it is stated by all the Irish annalists, and it may, therefore, be considered as a historical truth, that Donogh O'Brien, being deposed by his nephew, Turlogh, whose father he had caused to be murdered, went, in 1063 (not 1023) on a perpetual pilgrimage to Rome, where he died, after much penance and remorse, in the Church of St. Stephen, the protomartyr; but it is nowhere stated that he carried with him 'the harp and other regalia of his father;' nor is it likely that he would have been allowed to do so, though he might have been permitted to carry away his own crown. The crown and other regalia of the celebrated Brian were most probably lost to the Momonians at the Battle of Clontarf, when that old military usurper was slain by the Danes; for it is on record that his sceptre was found there in the beginning of the last century. It is, indeed, stated in Mac Geoghegan's translation of the Book of Clonmacnoise

Engraved by John Kirkwood Dublin

Ancient Irish Harp in Trinity College Dublin
Left Hand Side View

Published by Hodges & Smith Dublin

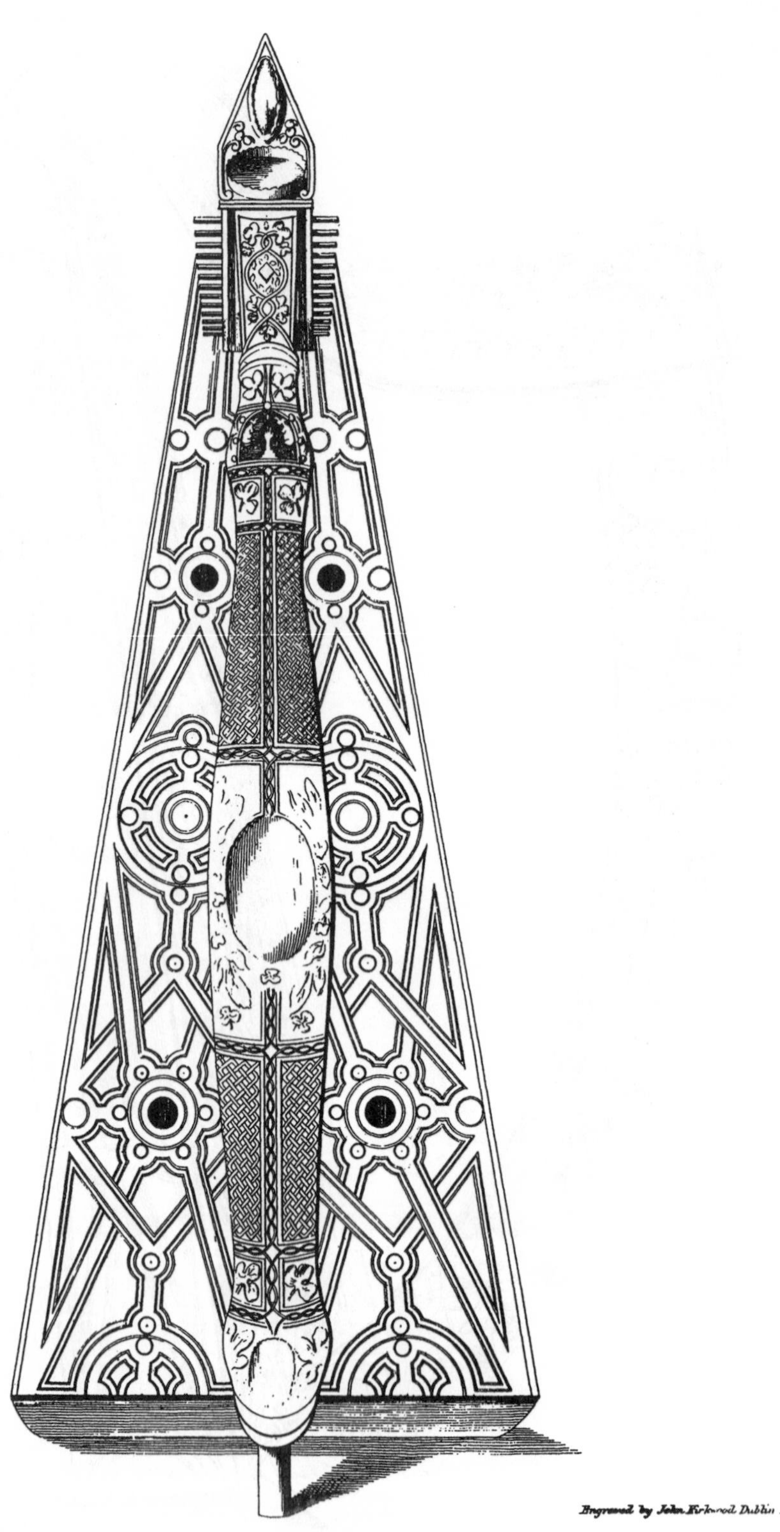

Engraved by John Kirkwood Dublin.

Ancient Irish Harp in Trinity College Dublin
Front View

Published by Hodges & Smith Dublin

that 'Donchad carried with him to Rome the crown of Ireland, which the Popes kept, until Pope Adrian gave the same to Henry II. that conquered Ireland.' But even this authority is at variance with the statement in the legend, according to which both harp and crown were preserved at Rome till the reign of Henry VIII., and which attributes to the Pope the characteristic prudence of retaining for himself the crown, 'which was of massive gold.' As, however, the averment in Mac Geoghegan, whose work is full of the translator's interpolations, is not corroborated by the authority of any of the old annalists, and as its untruth in one particular, the gift of the crown to Henry II., is quite certain,—for it was not a crown, but a gold ring with an emerald set in it, that Adrian sent him,—both statements, Mac Geoghegan's no less than O'Gorman's, must alike be given up as of no value. Such, indeed, is the view taken of the matter by our best historian, as well as poet, Moore, who thus expresses himself on the subject:

" 'According to some writers this royal pilgrim (Donchad) took away with him to Rome the crown of Ireland and laid it at the feet of the Pope; and it is certain that instances were by no means uncommon of princes laying, in those times, their crowns and kingdoms at the feet of the Popes, and receiving them back as fiefs of the Holy See. But, besides that in none of our authentic annals is any mention made of such an act of Donchad, it does not appear how the crown of Ireland could have been disposed of by him, having never, in fact, been in his possession; and his own crown of Munster he had, previously to his departure, transferred to his nephew's brow. The tale was most probably, therefore, invented in after times, either for the purpose of lending a colour to the right assumed by Pope Adrian of bestowing the sovereignty of Ireland on Henry II., or, at a still later period, for the very different purpose of furnishing Irishmen with the not inconvenient argument, that if former Popes possessed the power of bestowing on the English the right of sovereignty over Ireland, there appeared no reason whatever why future Popes should not give back the dominion to its first rightful owners.'

"It is scarcely necessary to pursue the examination of this story further, except, perhaps, to remark that the allegations in it respecting the gift of the harp from the Pope to King Henry VIII., and again from King Henry to the Earl of Clanricarde, have no better authority to rest on than that of the chevalier himself. There is, however, one statement appended to the story, as an evidence of its truth, which should not be passed over in silence, as it exhibits in an equal degree the antiquarian ignorance and the daring mendacity of the writer: this statement is, that on the front arm of the harp 'are chased in silver the arms of the O'Brien family; the bloody hand supported by lions.' As already remarked by Mr. Moore, the circumstance of arms being on the instrument is fatal to its reputed antiquity, as the hereditary use of armorial ensigns was not introduced into Europe until the time of the Crusades, and was not established in England until the reign of Henry III. The statement, however, is altogether erroneous: the supporters are not lions, but dogs, probably wolf-dogs, and the arms are not those of the O'Brien family, but of the more illustrious sept of O'Neil; and it is an interesting circumstance in the history of this harp, that the person who last awoke its long dormant harmonies was a minstrel descended from the same royal race to whom it originally owed its existence, the celebrated Arthur O'Neill having played it through the streets of Limerick in the year 1760.

"The legend so long connected with this interesting relic being now disposed of, it only remains to inquire, I. To what age the instrument really belongs; and, II. Whether it was originally intended for secular or for ecclesiastical purposes. The first question might be determined by the skilful antiquary with sufficient accuracy, from the style of workmanship of the armorial bearings already noticed, which evidently belongs to the close of the fourteenth, or, more probably, to the early part of the fifteenth century; and the general character of the interlaced ornaments on the harp, though derived from an earlier age, also points to the same period. But, though hitherto unnoticed, there is one feature observable among those ornaments which decides this question with still greater certainty, namely, the letters I. H. S. carved in relievo in the Gothic or black letter character, in general use at that period, and which is not found on monuments of an earlier age.

"That this harp did not belong to the class of bardic instruments, but rather to that smaller class used chiefly by the Irish ecclesiastics as accompaniments to their voices in singing their hymns, would seem most probable from its very small size, which would unfit it for being used by the minstrel at the festive board; and this conclusion seems to acquire support from the sacred monogram already noticed as being carved upon it. That harps of this description were in common use among the Irish ecclesiastics from the very introduction of Christianity into this country is sufficiently apparent from the lives of the most distinguished of the Irish saints, as well as from the testimony of Cambrensis in the twelfth century. 'Hinc accidit, ut Episcopi et abbates, et sancti in Hiberniâ viri cytharas circumferre et in eis modulando piè delectari consueverunt.'—*Cambriæ Descrip.* p. 739. Harps of this description are represented on the knees of ecclesiastics on several of our ancient stone crosses of the eighth, ninth, and tenth centuries, and also appear on some of our ancient shrines and reliquaries of later date, as on an ancient shrine, apparently of the eleventh century, in the possession of the writer, and on a beautiful reliquary preserved in the west of Ireland, popularly called *Fiachal Phadruig*, or Patrick's Tooth; the figures on which, as appears from an inscription, were executed at the expense of the Lord Thomas de Bramigham, Lord of Athenry, in the early part of the fourteenth century.

"If, then, conjecture were allowed, it would not perhaps be altogether an improbable surmise that this harp was made for one of those two O'Neills who flourished in the fourteenth century, the first as Bishop of Clogher, and the second as Bishop of Derry. But, however this may be, as a specimen of the harp in use among our early ecclesiastics, it will be impossible to avoid regarding it as a most interesting and valuable remain; and it may be hoped that every care will be taken to preserve it from further decay, as a truly national monument of antiquity."

From recent examination it appears that this harp had but one row of strings; that these were thirty in number, not twenty-eight, as was formerly supposed; thirty being the number of brass tuning pins and of corresponding string-holes. It is thirty-two inches high, and of exquisite workmanship: the upright pillar is of oak, and the sound-board of red sallow; the extremity of the forearm or harmonic curved bar is capped in part with silver, extremely well wrought and chiselled. It also contains a large crystal set in silver, under which was another stone, now lost. The buttons or ornamental knobs at the sides of the curved bar are of silver. The string-holes of the sound-board are neatly ornamented with escutcheons of brass carved and gilt. The four sounding-holes have also had ornaments probably of silver, as they have been the object of theft. The bottom which it rests upon is a little broken, and the wood very much decayed. The whole bears evidence of having been the work of a very expert artist. As it is unquestionably the most ancient harp in existence, the Editor has had drawings of it executed with a degree of care and accuracy suitable to its important character. One of these, a right-hand side view, forms the frontispiece to this chapter; the others, a left-hand side view, and a front view, will be found annexed to Mr. Petrie's memoir.* In the two latter, the artist has left his work in outline, for the purpose of exhibiting more distinctly the minute and beautiful carving which on all parts of the instrument attests the high state of the ornamental arts in Ireland at this period.

There is a peculiar elegance in the form of this beautiful instrument, which cannot fail to strike the eye of every one conversant with drawing, and which, taken in connexion with the striking similarity of the ornaments at the head and foot of the forearm, will at once recal to the mind of the musical inquirer the alleged harp of Queen Mary,[a] in Mr. Gunn's

[a] The following reasons are submitted for doubting the accuracy of Mr. Gunn's information concerning this instrument. Mr. Gunn states that "Queen Mary, in a hunting excursion in the Highlands of Perthshire, had taken with her this harp, and had made a present of it to Miss Beatrix Gardyn, daughter of Mr. Gardyn of Banchory, whose family is now represented by Mr. Gardyn of Troup. This lady having been married into the family of Lude (Robertson) cadet of the Clan Donnachy, the harp has remained in its possession until the present time. It had in front of the upper arm the queen's portrait and the arms of Scotland, both in gold, of which it was despoiled in the rebellion of 1745."—(General Robertson's Letter to the Secretary of the Highland Society, Oct. 1805.) As to the portrait of the queen having originally adorned the forearm, it is submitted that little reliance can be placed on a tradition half a century old, concerning so vague a matter as the likeness of a portrait; and that as to the emblazonment of the royal arms, such was customary on harps belonging to private individuals: thus the royal arms appear surmounting those of Fitzgerald on the Dallway harp. These objections would, however, be of little weight, if the story, as stated above, were consistently affirmed; but, so far from this being the case, it appears from a subsequent part of Mr. Gunn's work, (p. 78,) that the statement as to Miss Gardyn's supposed marriage into the house of Lude was a mistake; that she was really married, not to a Robertson, but to Findlay More Farquarson, of Invercauld, and that the harp is supposed to have come to Lude with some of her female descendants. Here, it must be admitted, is a material break in the chain connecting the harp of Beatrix Gardyn with that under consideration, inasmuch as it no longer distinctly appears either how or when the latter got into the possession of the Robertsons. Mr. Gunn himself seems to have had some misgivings on the subject, for he remarks on the inconsistency of Queen Mary, who was skilled in the musical science, not of the *Celtic*, but of the *Italian* school, having such an instrument. (p. 75.) So far, we have only stated matters

*[In this Dover edition, the left and front views appear between pages 40 and 41.]

Historical Enquiry, an instrument which contrasts very favourably with the heavy and coarse harp of the Lamonts, represented in the same volume, and designated as the "Caledonian harp."

calculated to weaken the force of the Lude tradition, as relied on by Mr. Gunn. If enough has been shewn to create a reasonable doubt of its authenticity, the following more positive evidences will be perused with considerable interest. Rory Dall O'Cahan, of whom some notice will be found in another part of this volume, was a famous Irish harper, who travelled into Scotland in the beginning of the seventeenth century, where he became celebrated for the composition of *Purths*, or harp lessons. Purth Gordon, Purth Atholl, Purth Lennox, and numerous other fine pieces, were composed by him, in compliment to his various entertainers, for he was himself a man of rank, and was honourably received in the houses of the chief nobility and gentry. But there is no mention whatever of Rory Dall *O'Cahan* among the writers on Scottish music, though they all notice a Rory Dall *Morison* as flourishing at that period, and as being the last of the old race of Scottish harpers.—(Macdonald's Essay, p. 11; Gunn's Inquiry, pp. 95, 97; Dauney's Ancient Melodies of Scotland, p. 84, &c.) Now if it should appear that the Irish tradition is so corroborated as to leave no doubt of its truth, it must be concluded that Morison was either an assumed or an imputed name, and that the accounts of all parties refer to the same individual. But the Irish tradition is proved thus: "Roger," says Arthur O'Neill, relating what he had heard of O'Cahan, "died in Scotland, in a nobleman's house, where he left his harp and silver key to tune it. A blind harper, named Echlin Kane, a scholar of Lyons, whom I often met, and an excellent harper, afterwards went over to Scotland, and called at the house where Roger's harp and key were, and the heir of the deceased nobleman took a liking to Echlin, and made him a present of the silver key, he being namesake to its former owner; but the dissipated rascal sold it in Edinburgh, and drank the money."—(MS. Autobiography of Arthur O'Neill, *penes* the Editor.) The Editor had this tale from O'Neill in 1792, and also from Hempson, who had been taught by an O'Cahan, and lived in the O'Cahan country. Doctor M'Donnell, of Belfast, had heard the same story from O'Neill, when a boy, which carries it back to a period anterior to the publication of Dr. Johnson's Tour in the Hebrides, (1773,) in which the anecdote is alluded to; so that O'Neill's information must be held to be genuine, both as regards the suspicion of his having got it either from that work, or from Mr. Gunn's Essay, which was published in 1807, and which thus corroborates the testimony of the Irish harpers, and authenticates the adventures of O'Cahan in Scotland. "The celebrated performer, O'Kane," that is, Echlin, "had been about that time (1773) in the Highlands, and had frequently entertained the late Lord Macdonald with his excellent performances on the harp, at his lordship's residence in the Isle of Skye. There had been for a great length of time in the family a valuable *harp key*; it was finely ornamented with gold and silver, and with a precious stone: this key is said to have been worth eighty or a hundred guineas, and on this occasion our itinerant harper had the good fortune of being presented by Lord Macdonald with this curious and valuable implement of his profession."—(p. 48.) That Morison and O'Cahan were the same person must, therefore, be concluded. If any difficulty should arise from the name *Morison*, it may perhaps be obviated from the fact, that Gorry (or Godred) was a family name among the O'Cahans, and that a Highlander, speaking of Rory Dall, the son of Gorry, would say, not *Rory Dall an Gorrison*, but *Rory Dall an M(G)orrison*, the G in composition being eclipsed by M. At the same time, it must be admitted that there is no proof of Rory Dall being the son of a Gorry O'Cahan, although from the occurrence of the name in the inquisitions of this period, which are extremely vague and unsatisfactory, such a relationship is probable. It will be observed, that the story, as told by Mr. Gunn, says nothing of the harp being preserved along with the key; and indeed it is the only uncertainty in O'Neill's account, in which allowance must be made for the vagueness of traditionary story in one country about events occurring in another, that he makes the nobleman give away the key, while he kept the harp to which it was adapted. The inference from Mr. Gunn's account, that in 1773 there was no harp adapted to this key in Lord Macdonald's possession, would therefore appear the more probable. Either, then, O'Cahan's harp had left the Macdonald family, and been carried elsewhere, or the key alone had found its way to Skye, sometime after O'Cahan's death. The latter conclusion seems the more probable, for it is less likely that the owner of both harp and key should part with the former than

We also find the Irish harp, when first assumed as the national arms, designed precisely on the same model. Thus, in the national arms sketched on the map of Ireland, appended to the State Papers, vol. ii., and executed in the year 1567.

It is true, the Irish harp had appeared more than thirty years previously, on the coins of King Henry VIII., but the instrument there represented is probably figured more according to the fancy of the artist than the original,[a] for it bears a form different from that of any Irish harp that has been preserved, resembling more the common Italian harp of twenty-four strings, then in use, as represented in the Dodecachordon of Glareanus.—(*Basiliæ*, 1547.)

The harp called Brian Boru's may, therefore, be taken as the model, at least as to form, on which the Irish harp was constructed down to the seventeenth century, and as its admitted antiquity carries it back beyond the time of Galilei, and Galilei's testimony agrees with that

the latter. We are, therefore, led to seek for O'Cahan's harp elsewhere. Now we find Rory Dall at the house of Lude about the year 1650, composing one of his best *purths*, in honour of the ancestor of General Robertson. "Roderick Morison, one of the last native Highland harpers, who was regularly bred, and professionally instructed, accompanied the Marquis of Huntly on a visit to Lude, about the year 1650. This bard and harper composed a *port* or air on this occasion, which was called *Suipar Chiurn na Leod*, or Lude's Supper."—(Gunn, p. 91.) "Lude's Super, by Rory Dall," is published in Daniel Dow's Collection of Scottish Airs; and it is very remarkable, that of all the pieces formerly played on the harp in question by General Robertson's great-grandfather, who was the last person who performed on it, this very *purth* of Rory Dall's is now the only one remembered in the family, the only piece of musical tradition which still clings to the harp—shall we say, *of its composer?* Certainly the Irish appearance of the instrument, the visit of Rory Dall at Lude in his old age, the traditionary connexion of the harp with this particular *purth*, and the difficulty which attends the story of Miss Gardyn, would lead most minds to hesitate before rejecting such conclusions. It is worthy of remark, that this harp also, according to the drawing, has thirty strings.

[a] As on all our coinage, at least since the time of the Commonwealth.

of Dante, which, supported by the sculpture on the *Fiachail Phadruigh*, and by the drawing in the MS. of Cambrensis, extends backward to within a comparatively short time of the Anglo-Norman invasion; we are thus enabled to affirm, that from A.D. 1621, the time of the construction of the magnificent Dallway harp, of which a representation is given in a former volume of this work, back to the year 1180, there is no period of a century without evidence demonstrative of the fact that the Irish possessed a harp of sufficient compass for the performance of all our best harp airs with the appropriate basses. It is therefore concluded, as to this branch of the inquiry, that the genuine Irish harp in use at the beginning of the present century corresponds, if not in size, at least in compass, with the instrument used at the time of the Anglo-Norman invasion.

Assuming, then, that the Irish, in the latter end of the twelfth century, possessed an instrument fit for the performance of such harp airs as were then known, with their appropriate basses, we come next to inquire, how long had they possessed it? For, as Guido, of Arezzo, the inventor, or at least revivor of counterpoint among the Italians, lived somewhat more than a century before that time, a suspicion reasonably arises that they may have had their acquaintance with their improved style and method of playing from continental instruction. In answering the question proposed, and clearing away the preliminary objections, we draw our first assistance from the evidence of the Welsh. They, as is well known, had their musical canon regulated by Irish harpers, about A. D. 1100. This they would hardly have submitted to, had they not considered their instructors the greater proficients in the art, and yet the Welsh had before this time been noted for singing and performing in concert. But it may be objected by that numerous class, who would refer every thing creditable among the ancient Irish to a Danish origin, (confounding the Danes of the middle ages with the Tuath de Danans of tradition,) that they were Danish-Irish to whom Griffith ap Conan referred for these instructions, namely, to Aulaf, King of Dublin, the son of Sitrick; and that, of the harpers sent by the Hiberno-Danish monarch, one only, Mathuloch Gwyddell, is mentioned as Irish, while the chief musician, Olar Gerdawwr, is manifestly one of the Ostmen. To this it may be answered, that there is no trace of northern phraseology either in the Irish or Welsh musical nomenclature, but that, on the contrary, much, if not all, even of the Welsh vocabulary, is pure Irish.[a] Farther, that the harp, known from time immemorial to the Irish as *Cruit* and *Clarseach*, has never borne its Teutonic designation of *Hearpa* in any other of the languages of the United Kingdom than the English; and, finally, that these musical congresses, so far from being confined to the Danes of Dublin, were customary among the native Irish; for, not to dwell on similar assemblies at an earlier period, we find that a meeting, identical in its character and objects, was held before an Irish petty King, at Glendaloch, immediately after the one in question, at which the regulations of the Welsh synod were confirmed.[b]

But, fortunately, the question rests on evidence of a more tangible nature than mere

[a] See vol. i. of this work.

[b] Welsh Archæology, vol. iii. p. 625.

historical statement. Two monuments, one of the eleventh, and the other of a much earlier century, are now to be submitted, on which we have authentic contemporaneous delineations of the Irish harp executed by Irish artists.

The first is the ornamental cover or "theca" of an Irish manuscript, containing, among other writings, a liturgy of the seventh century, now preserved at Stowe, in the library of the Duke of Buckingham, and elaborately described by Doctor Charles O'Connor, in his Catalogue of the MSS. of this magnificent collection.[a] The age of the ornamental cover is ascertained by the inscriptions remaining on it, from which it appears to have been made by Donnachad O'Tagan, an artificer of the Irish monastery of Clonmacnoise, for Donchad, the son of Brian, King of Ireland, and for Maccraith O'Donnchad, King of Cashel, during the lifetime and reign of the former, and probably during the lifetime of the latter also. But it is stated in the Annals of Tighearnach that Donchad was expelled from the sovereignty in the year 1064, and died the year after, and that Maccraith, King of Cashel, died in 1052. The "theca" must therefore have been executed prior at least to the year 1064. Now among the ornaments of this cover are five delineations of the harp of that period, containing, however, two pairs of duplicates, *fac similes* of which are given at the end of the second volume of O'Connor's *Rerum Hibernicarum Scriptores Veteres*, whence the subjoined engravings have been accurately copied.

The first, probably owing to the minuteness of the scale on which it is engraved on the silver plate of the *theca*, is unsatisfactory as to the shape of the instrument, which appears not of a triangular, but of a quadrangular form, and is represented with only two strings, the latter feature being, however, a manifest defect in the drawing. It is nevertheless valuable, as showing that the mode of holding and playing on the instrument had altered in nothing from the practice of the eleventh century, at the time when the MS. of Cambrensis, already alluded to, was illustrated.

The harps in the second ornament are represented on a larger scale, but still not sufficiently so to enable the artist to show more than four or five strings on each. This piece of early Irish art, which combines embossing, enamelling, jewelling, and engraving, is thus

[a] Vol. i. Appen. i.

*

described by Doctor O'Connor: "Of the three central ornaments (i. e. of each marginal side) two are plates of silver; the third is the brazen image of a man dressed in a tunica, tightly fitted to his body, girdled round the waist and reaching to the knees. The legs and feet are bare, the hands and arms are also bare, and are extended round two harps, which support the arms on either side. The heads of the harp resemble in shape a small *Cornu Ammonis* of blue enamelled glass, and in the breast of the figure a small square hole is filled with a garnet."[a] These Cornua Ammonis would appear, however, rather to belong to the surrounding ornamental work than to the harps themselves, which otherwise correspond in their general form in a remarkable manner with the harp of Arthur O'Neill, as shown in the engraving of that interesting person. These, and the sculptured harp on the monument at Nieg, in Rosshire,[b] are the earliest extant delineations, so far as the knowledge of the writer extends, of the perfect harp, constructed with sounding board, fore pillar, and harmonic curve.[c]

The instrument submitted to the reader from the other monument above referred to is evidently of a much older date. The musical inquirer and general antiquary cannot fail to regard it with interest; *for it is the first specimen of the harp without a fore pillar that has hitherto been discovered out of Egypt*; and but for the recent confirmation of Bruce's testimony with regard to its Egyptian prototypes, might perhaps be received with equal incredulity; for, to the original difficulty of supposing such an instrument capable of supporting the tension of its strings, is now added the startling presumption that the Irish have had their harp originally out of Egypt.

[a] Stowe Cat. vol. i. App. p. 35.

[b] Cordner's Views of Ruins in North Britain.

[c] Doctor Ledwich, as might be expected, insists that the pillar at Nieg is a Danish monument; but he assigns no reason whatever for the assertion, farther than, that the figure of a bird (the *rafn*, of course) appears at the top of the sculpture, and that the part of the country where it is found was much visited by Scandinavian pirates. At this rate, there are few monuments in Christendom which could not be proved to be the work of the same people.

The drawing is taken from one of the ornamental compartments of a sculptured cross, at the old Church of Ullard, in the County of Kilkenny. From the style of the workmanship, as well as from the worn condition of the cross, it seems older than the similar monument at Monasterboyce, which is known to have been set up before the year 830. The sculpture is rude; the circular rim which binds the arms of the cross together is not pierced in the quadrants, and many of the figures originally represented in relievo are now wholly abraded. It is difficult to determine whether the number of strings represented is six or seven; but, as has been already remarked, accuracy in this respect cannot be expected either in sculptures or in many picturesque drawings. One hand only of the performer is shown, it probably being beyond the art of the sculptor to exhibit the other, and this, which is the right hand, is stretched, as in all the preceding examples, towards the longer strings of the instrument. The harp is also held on the knee as in the other instances, the only difference between the sculpture here and the first engraving on the *theca* of the Stowe MS. being that the Ullard harp, to all appearance, has no front arm or pillar. In both cases the musician is naked, and yet both are associated with representations of churchmen and others in rich dresses; but it will be recollected that in the hands of the figure who appears clad in the ornamented tunic on the *theca*, there are represented harps of a perfect form, while that played on by the naked musician in the adjoining compartment is very rude in its structure, and strongly resembles the Ullard instrument. Hence we must by no means receive the latter as conclusive evidence that at the time of its being sculptured, there was no other description of harp in use.

An interesting speculation might here be indulged in, with respect both to the origin of the harp itself, and to the route by which it has found its way into the North and West of

Any one who desires to see specimens of Scandinavian art, of the tenth century, will find abundance in the recently published Antiquitates Americanæ, from which an opinion may be formed of the competency of that people to execute such works as the beautifully sculptured pillars and crosses copied by Mr. Cordiner. This rage for assigning every thing Irish to the Danes is, perhaps, the most absurd method that we Irish have yet discovered for showing our political and polemical animosities. Had Doctor Ledwich not been under the influence of *Danomania*, when he wrote respecting the pillar at Nieg, he would have recollected that, centuries before the Scandinavian incursions, this very district was the scene of Scotic colonization. The writer of the ancient life of St. Cadroe (quoted in Pinkerton's Vitæ Sanctorum Scotiæ) states, that the Scots, after coming from Ireland, and occupying Iona, crossed the adjoining sea to the mainland, and, going over the river Ross, occupied the region of Rossia, and settled there. Should it be objected, that the Ross here meant is not the present district of that name, the inquirer is referred to the Dublin University Magazine for October, 1837, p. 434, where the difficulties of supposing it any other than the Ross above mentioned are enumerated.

An honourable task remains for Scottish antiquaries, in elucidating the emblematic figures on these pillars. The unknown animal, which some will have to be a lamb, and others an elephant, and which is of such constant occurrence on these Scoto-Pictish monuments, appears on the Nieg pillar, just above the harp. It also forms a conspicuous object on the round tower at Brechin, which is unquestionably the work of Irish artificers. Its presence, therefore, on the monument in question does not impeach the probability of the harp there represented being the work of a Scotic sculptor in the Pictish times.

Europe. It is impossible to look at a side view of the old *testudo*, without at once perceiving the similarity between it, taken in that aspect, and the one-armed Egyptian harp; for the shell corresponds in all respects to the sounding chamber of the Theban instrument, and the horn to its curved arm,—the only difference consisting in this, that the strings of the *testudo* are extended from the shell to a cross bar fixed between two horns, whereas in the harp, the strings are extended from the sounding chamber directly to the arm itself, the flexure of which, corresponding to that in the horn, forms pretty nearly an harmonic curve. In a word, it would appear as if the Egyptian harp were no more than a single-horned *testudo*, enlarged by the substitution of a wooden chamber and wooden curved upright respectively, for the tortoise shell and goat's horn, which appear to have been the principal materials used in the construction of the original *cithara*. This conjecture receives a certain amount of confirmation from the classic fable which represents Mercury as having found the tortoise, from the shell of which he framed the first *cithara*, among the mud of the receding Nile. Now, the transition from the Theban harp to that at present in use is by no means difficult to be traced. The introduction of a front arm, suggested by the very defects of the instrument, would reduce it to a shape corresponding very closely with the quadrilateral harp represented on the *theca* of the Stowe MS. The incorporation of the sounding chamber with the other upright would, by an equally obvious improvement, bring it precisely to the modern model: and indeed we are entitled to assume that it has passed through these gradations, from the fact of finding specimens of the instrument in both stages of improvement in our own country. The *cithara*, then, being admittedly the parent of the lute and violin, and there appearing such grounds for regarding it as the parent also of the one-armed harp, which again seems by so natural a transition to pass into the form of harp now in use, we have an explanation of the difficulty which every inquirer on these subjects must have felt, from finding the Irish harp and the British viol, instruments at present so very dissimilar in point of form, bearing the common appellation of *cruit*.

Should these grounds appear sufficient for the surmise that the harp is really a variety of the *cithara* or *testudo*, derived through an Egyptian channel, the importance of our bardic tradition of the progress of the early colonists of Ireland from Egypt through Scythia, will at once be apparent. There can be no question of the fact, that, at a very early period, a strong tide of civilization flowed into the East of Europe from the Nile, and thence spread Northward and Westward; and there are many grounds extrinsic to this inquiry, on which it appears that a strong argument may be raised for intimate international relations between the original inhabitants of these islands and the ancient occupants of the East of Europe. If the various points of resemblance, and even identity, on which such an argument might be rested, were adduced, it would probably appear something more than a coincidence, that in a monument erected at Petau, in Stiria, during the life of the Emperor Aurelius, the Thracian Orpheus should be represented performing on an instrument in all respects resembling that on the *theca* of the Stowe MS. (*Montfauçon*, v. i. p. 252,) being in fact what has just been surmised to be the Egyptian harp in its transition state, after it had received its forearm, and before it had acquired its perfect triangular form by the incorporation of the sounding chamber with the other upright.

But, to return to the more immediate subject of inquiry.—There being two descriptions of harp in use in the eleventh century, the one a rude and apparently quadrilateral instrument in the hands of a naked performer, the other a perfectly formed harp in those of a richly dressed individual, it might be surmised that we had here the *Clarseach* and *Cruit* accurately distinguished; but so far as the writer can observe, the word *Clarseach* is rather a modern synonyme for Cruit, than an original specific name for the harp, as distinguished from that instrument. *Cruit* is the word commonly employed to designate the harp in our annals, and even in modern compositions. Thus Keating, the historian, addressing Thadeus O'Coffey, a celebrated performer on the harp, who lived about the beginning of the seventeenth century, when the Cruit, if ever it was different from the harp in Ireland, was forgotten, asks,

> Cia an saoí le seinntir an ċruit?
> le moċtar neiṁ go nuaḋ luit
> Tré ġoireaḋ guṫ-binn a colar
> Mar sruiṫ-binn ḟoġar orgáin?

"Who is the artist by whom the harp (cruit) is played? by whom the anguish of the envenomed spear's recent wound is healed, through the sweet-voiced sound of the sounding-board, (*clar*,) like the sweet streamed peal of the organ?" &c.

Hence it will be necessary to guard also against interpreting *Cruit* and *Cruitiré* as applying only to an inferior description of harp and harper; for, as the names *Clarseach* and *Clarseachair* seem to have come into use in Irish writings long subsequent to the age of Cambrensis, we are left to conduct any further speculations, as to the form and compass of the Irish harp, on the evidence only of such mention of it, and its professors, as occurs in the annals and ecclesiastical writings under the former names, or those of *Cithara* and *Citharista*.

Cambrensis states that the Northumbrians of his time sung in two parts, a fact also remarked by Beda; and these Northumbrians, it is well known from the latter authority, had been converted to Christianity by Irish monks, under the rule of Colman, a disciple of the Monastery of Bangor, in the county of Down. Now, Colman, the christianizer of the Northumbrians, and subsequently the founder of the College of Mayo of the Saxons, was the immediate predecessor of Columbanus, whose *regula cœnobialis*, or rule for conventual exercises, founded on the practice of the parent house at Bangor, contains express directions for the singing of the psalter by the household in choirs,[a] as noticed by Doctor Ledwich in his learned treatise in Walker's Bards. In truth, it was from these choirs that Bangor itself took its name.[b] Antiphonial singing was also practised in the same monastery, as early as the Northumbrian Mission, and the very Antiphonary of Bangor itself is still preserved in a MS. of the seventh century at Bobio, in Italy,[c] alluding to which, Gerebert says, when speaking of the propagation of Christianity among the German nations in that age, "To this epoch we may refer the antiphonary of the monastery of Bangor, whence St. Columbanus, coming forth with St. Abbo, his companion, not only imbued our Germany with the light of the Christian faith, but also with the principles of ascetic living." "Doubtless," he continues, "the first rule for arranging ecclesiastical services among us, as made up of psalms, canticles, hymns, collects, and antiphonies, was hence derived."[d] Usher and Mabillon cite, with regard to the same choral service of Bangor, a tract, *De Cursuum Ecclesiasticorum Origine,* first noticed by Spelman, and of which there was extant a manuscript copy nine hundred years old at the time when Usher wrote (1639.) This tract states as follows: "Saint Jerome affirms that the same service (*cursum*) which is performed at the present time (i. e. in the seventh century) by the Scots, was chaunted likewise by Saint Mark. Patrick, when placed by Lupus and Germanus as archbishop over the Scots and Britons, chaunted the same service there, and, after him, Saint Wandilochus Senex and Saint Comogill, who had about three thousand in their monastery, (chaunted it also.) Saint Wandilochus being thence sent forth as a preacher by Saint Comogill, as also Saint Columbanus, they arrived at Louvaine, in Gaul, and there they chaunted the same service, and thence the fame of their sanctity was spread abroad over the earth, &c.; and thus that (service) which St. Mark the Evangelist had once chaunted was revived again under the blessed Columbanus."[e] However apochryphal the apostolic antiquity thus assigned to the choral service of Bangor, the evidence as to its use in and before the seventh century is unquestionable, and invests every fragment of it that has come down to us with a very high degree of historic interest. The whole Antiphonary is preserved, and is given, together with a hymn entitled "Memoria Patrum Nostrorum," by Muratori in his Ambrosian Anecdotes, and by O'Connor in the first volume of his *Rerum Hibernicarum Scriptores.* Both are composed in perfect rhyme, as well as in regular rythm; as a specimen of which, a verse in praise of Bangor is subjoined, from the Antiphonary.

[a] "Totum psalterium inter duas supradictas noctes numero cantent, *duodecim choris* * * * Ad initium vero noctis duodecim psalmi similiter *psalluntur* * * * Sub uno cursu 75 (psalmi) cantantur."—(Reg. Mon. Ed. Sirini, c. vii. p. 6.) The fourth chapter is, "De eo qui in exordio psalmi non bene cantaverit." (p. 20.) See Rer. Hib. Scrip. Vet. v. i. p. clxiv.; Anec. Ambros. p. 121.

[b] ƀan choıṗ, the fair choir; or ƀen choıṗ, tho head choir.

[c] Muratori. Anec. t. iv. p. 121.

[d] Gerebert Mus. Sac. v. i. p. 164-5.

[e] Ussher Primord p. 342; Mabillon de Liturg. Gal. 384.

Virgo valde fœcunda	A virgin very fruitful
Hac et mater intacta,	Is she—a mother chaste—
Læta et tremebunda	Joyful all and fearful
Verbo Dei subacta.	In God's own arms embrac'd.

Thus it appears that long before the appearance of rhyme in the compositions of Continental writers, the Irish ecclesiastics of Bangor were acquainted with the choral performance of rythmical hymns.

That this was the source from which the Northumbrians drew their knowledge of singing in parts may, therefore, be affirmed with no slight degree of confidence; especially when it is recollected that Bangor was for centuries the chief town of that district, in which our peasantry retain the practice of singing in parts to this day. Strange, indeed, if the homely air of "Ballinderry,"[a] to which so many rude and ludicrous verses have been from time to time adapted by the peasantry of Down and Antrim, from Magheralin to Portglenone, be really a relic of that illustrious school of music and theology from which the churches of Northumberland, Mercia, Germany, Franconia, Burgundy, and Switzerland,[b] drew their knowledge, not only of ecclesiastical discipline and service, but of the Christian faith itself!

But traces of choral service appear in even an earlier age than that of the Northumbrian missionaries. There are extant Latin hymns of Columba, composed soon after the middle of the sixth century, which furnish strong reasons for believing that divine service was chaunted in concert by his household also, at Iona, thus:

Protegat nos altissimus	May the High and Holy One
De suis sanctis sedibus	Guard us from His Heavenly Throne,
Dum ibi hymnos canimus	While we sing, with grateful hearts,
Decem statutis vicibus.[c]	Hymns in ten appointed parts.

It does not positively appear, so far as the knowledge of the writer extends, that the harp, although a favourite instrument with the clergy in Cambrensis's time, was made use of as an accompaniment in these performances; but such an inference may be drawn from the use of the word *psalluntur*, indicating an instrumental accompaniment, in the rule of Columbanus, organs not having been in use in church worship until the century after.[d] It may also be remarked, that, until a comparatively recent period, the harp was the usual accompaniment of the mass in our country districts. Should it appear from these considerations probable that it had a place in the early choirs of Bangor and Iona, it will afford grounds for a very confident conjecture, that at the period in question it had compass enough for a regular performance in parts.

That it was used with the voice in performances in concert in the tenth century, and was then believed to have been customarily so used, even so far back as the fifth, appears

[a] See Preface, p. 8. [b] See O'Connor, Stowe Cat. Appendix ii. [c] Colgan. Trias. Thaum., p. 476.

[d] The burning of the organs of Cluaincrema, in Ireland, is mentioned in the Annals of Ulster, A. D. 814.

clearly from the following passage in the life of St. Brigid, by Animchad or Animosus, Bishop of Kildare, who died A. D. 980.

"The blessed virgin on another occasion was requested to go to the king of that country, (Munster,) who was then at the plain of Cliach, for the purpose of procuring the liberation of a certain person whom the king had in chains. So the beloved of Christ came to the king's house, but did not find the king there; the fosterfather of the king, however, with certain of his friends, were in the house. And the blessed virgin, seeing harps in the house, said, 'Play upon your harps to us;' (*Citharizate nobis.*) They answered her, 'Lady, the harpers are not now in the house.' Then one of the companions of the holy Bridget, speaking jestingly, said to them, 'Let the holy virgin bless your hands, in order that you may be enabled to perform what she desires of you, and obey her directions.' Then the king's fosterfather and his sons said, 'Let, then, the holy one of God give us her blessing, so that we may play upon our harps for her;' (*Citharizemus ei.*) And the saint having blessed them, they took the harps, and, ignorant though they were, yet they played upon the harps sweetly and in modulation, as if they had been skilful harpers. (*Et modulanter rudes, quasi periti citharistæ, et dulciter citharizabant.*) Then the king came to the house, and, hearing the sound of the song, (*carminis,*) asked 'Who sings?' (*quis facit hoc carmen?*) and one meeting him said, 'My lord, your fosterfather and his sons (are they who sing) at the command of the holy Brigid.' The king, astonished at the fact, entered the house, and straightway craved a blessing of the saint," &c. He liberates his prisoner, in consideration of the blessing which he receives, and the adventure ends thus:—"But the king's fosterfather and his sons were approved harpers, even unto the day of their death, and their descendants (*nepotes*) were the honored (*venerabiles*) harpers of kings."[a]

In like manner, the author of the very ancient life of St. Kiaran states of Angus, King of Munster, whose death is mentioned in the Ulster Annals, A. D. 489, that he had excellent harpers, who, playing upon their harps before him, sung the acts of heroes sweetly in verse; (*in carmine citharizantes canebant.*)[b]

So also Dallan Forgall, in his poem on the death of his cotemporary, Columba, who died A. D. 594:

Is aḃran re cruit gan ceis—sinde deis air n argain uais.

"The song with (i. e. accompanied by) the harp, is without joy—a sound following the bier to the grave." Whence it appears, that in the sixth century the harp was also used as an accompaniment to the *caionan.*

Doubtless, the poet mentioned by Adamnan in his life of Columba,[c] as one who sung canticles in modulation according to the rules of his art, (*modulabiliter—ex more artis suæ,*) was a harper as well as singer; and although it is probably no more than a chance coincidence,

[a] Colgan Trias Thaum., pp. 557, 8; Ex vita iv. S. Brigidæ, c. 80.

[b] Capgrave Acta, SS. p. 460.

[c] Colgan Trias Thaum., p. 347.

it may be worth while to remark, that his name, Cronan, corresponds with the Irish term for the bass in music. Thus the rude species of counterpoint, accompanying the air of Ballinderry, is called its *Cronan*, even by the English and Scottish settlers of the present day.

Mention of the Cruit, but not associated with other music, occurs in the Irish poems ascribed to St. Columba; and, in the very ancient description of the Teach Mid Chuarta, or Hall of Tara, written probably in the sixth century, and referring to the manners of the third, a place is assigned, among the occupants of the various seats in the hall, to the *Cruitire* or harpers.[a]

To conclude the inquiry respecting this instrument, the following remarkable passage is submitted, from the Book of Lecan.[b] The opening poem of the collection, part of which is lost, embodies a series of triads metaphorically descriptive of the skill and power of the Tuath de Danaans, the predecessors of the alleged Milesian Colony, and a race to whom, undoubtedly, much of the ancient excellence of the arts in Ireland is to be attributed. The language employed, and the use of the triad, indicate, perhaps, a higher antiquity than that of any of the evidences above adduced. The triads are employed thus: "Blackness, Obscurity, and Darkness, were their (the Dedanaan's) three cup-bearers; Strength, Robustness, and Vigour, their three servants; Storm, Wind, and Breeze, their three horses; Indagation, Pursuit, and Swiftness, their three hounds," &c., the intention appearing in general to be, to assign a positive, comparative and superlative of each species, to each triad. That alluding to the present subject of inquiry is as follows: Ceol agus binn agus tétbinn tri cruitiri, i.e. as rendered in the old translation quoted by Mr. Hardiman,[c] "Music, Melody, and Harmony of Strings, were their three harpers." And this translation of tetbinn seems the correct one. But "harmony of strings," as expressing something more than "melody," can mean nothing but musical concord. With respect, therefore, to the Irish harp of the time of Cambrensis, it is submitted, that there appear sufficient grounds for supposing it to have been in use in this island from a period anterior to the arrival of the Scotic colony. Our harp tunes, requiring an instrument of a certain compass for their performance, have, consequently, as great a length of time through which to stretch back their claims on antiquity, as those the structure of which indicates a ruder origin; and thus the lament of Deirdre, and the other early pieces proper to the harp, in this collection, may assert their Ossianic and Pagan origin, unimpeded by the objection, that the Irish of that æra had no instrument capable of performing them. Indeed, if the testimony of Cambrensis were to be implicitly relied on, the harp tunes would be the only ones on which the high antiquity of Irish music could legitimately rest, for Cambrensis denies us the honor of the bagpipe,[d] which is manifestly the parent of almost all the airs of the other class.

[a] Petrie on the Antiquities of Tara Hill, Trans. R. I. A., vol. xviii. part 2, p. 187.

[b] Library, R. I. A.

[c] Irish Minstrelsy, vol. ii. p. 353.

[d] That the *chorus* of Giraldus is the bagpipe has been recently demonstrated in Mr. Dauney's learned work on ancient Scottish music.

But it would appear that the statement of the Bishop of St. David's must have been made on imperfect information. He states that the Irish used and took delight in two instruments, the harp and tympanum; while the Scotch used three, the harp, tympanum, and bagpipe. As to the tympanum, which has generally been supposed to be a drum, Doctor O'Connor[a] adduces an Irish poem, "certainly composed before the destruction of the Irish monarchy by the invasion of the Danes," in which the harper is directed to mind his *cruit*, and the minstrel the strings of his *tiompan*, or his *tiompan* of strings: whence it seems evident, as the learned writer shows, that this instrument was a species of lute or gittern; for, in a passage of Suetonius,[b] descriptive of a Gaul playing on it, it is further characterized as being round, and played on with the fingers; and it appears also from Ovid,[c] to have been covered with skin,—in a word, an instrument in all respects resembling a South Sea islander's guitar. It is very remarkable, that in Shane O'Neachtan's song of Maggy Laider,[d] an Irish composition of the seventeenth century, but now nearly naturalized in Scotland, this primitive instrument is introduced as an accompaniment of the bagpipe:

Seinn duin̄ steangcan, píob ar tiompan,
So an coiṁ-gair gleorach !

It is not probable, however, that so trifling an instrument could have had much influence on the music of a people possessing the harp, and, as we now proceed to show, the bagpipe also, from time immemorial.

The military music of a demi-barbarous people is much less likely to undergo alterations than their domestic music, so that the fact of the Irish and Scotch Highlanders having marched to the music of the bagpipe on their military expeditions, any time within memory, should be sufficient to lead to the *prima facie* presumption, that it had been in use among them immemorially. The pipes are admitted to have been the proper military music of the Irish shortly before the treaty of Limerick: it is now proposed to inquire how long they had possessed them before that epoch. In a contemporaneous drawing of the rout of O'Donnell and Tyrone at the battle of Ballyshannon, in A. D. 1593, preserved in the British Museum,[e] one piper is represented running away with the rest of the troops, and the pipes of another lie on the ground near him. The bag, which is held on the belly and squeezed by the fore-arm, is inflated from the mouth, and the instrument possesses a chanter and two drones. The drawing, which appears to have been made by a common soldier in the English army, is, however, too roughly executed to render it of much value as an illustration. A more satisfactory representation is found in the following very characteristic figure of an Irish piper of the same reign, but of an earlier date, given in the rare illustrations of Derrick's Image

[a] Catalogue of Stowe MSS. vol. i. p. 147. [b] In Aug. c. 68. [c] In Fastis, l. iv. v. 302.

[d] Mr. Hardiman, who gives the song in his Minstrelsy, had it from a copy made in the year 1706. The air and name have unquestionably been plagiarized by our neighbours.

[e] Aug. 2. 38.

of Ireland.—(*Imprinted at London by Ihon Daie*, 1581.) In the original wood-cut he appears heading a body of native Irish, who are employed in burning and pillaging a cabin on the borders of the Pale.

This plate is interesting, not only on account of the magnificent pipes on which the performer plays, but also as a specimen of native costume in the sixteenth century. We here see the flowing sleeves, and the glibb of the pure "merus Hibernicus." He wears armlets, and carries a sword; and in the next plate is represented as slain in the front of the battle, while his pipes lie on the ground beside him.

The instrument he carries is twice the ordinary size, and possesses a double drone and two chanters, on one of which, something resembling a rude representation of keys may be observed. The extremity of the mouthpiece, where inserted into the bag, is bushed with a tassel; and a similar provision is made against the escape of the wind at the insertion of the chanters.

The bag is suspended round the neck by a broad belt, passing over the right shoulder; and on the whole, the Kerne and his pipes make a fine barbaric appearance, probably in most respects identical with that displayed by the performer of Brian Boru's march five centuries before. That they are keys which are represented on the chanter is by no means impossible, for bagpipes of a very perfect construction inflated by bellows, and furnished with numerous keys, were at this time in use on the Continent.

Very interesting cotemporaneous notices of the bagpipe of this period, (first noticed by the late Henry Joy, Esq., in a learned paper in the *Dublin University Magazine* for July, 1833,) are found in Stanihurst and Galilei. The former, writing about 1584, says, "The Irish likewise, instead of the trumpet, make use of a wooden pipe of the most ingenious structure, to which is joined a leathern bag, very closely bound with bands. A pipe is inserted in the side of this skin, through which the piper, with his swollen neck and puffed up cheeks, blows in the same manner as we do through a tube. The skin, being thus filled with air, begins to swell, and the player presses against it with his arm; thus a loud and shrill sound is produced through two wooden pipes of different lengths. In addition to these, there is yet a fourth pipe, perforated in different places, which the player so regulates by the dexterity of his fingers, in the shutting and opening the holes, that he can cause the upper pipes to send forth either a loud or a low sound at pleasure. The principal thing to be taken care of, is, that the air be not allowed to escape through any other part of the bag than that in which the pipes are inserted. For, if any one were to make a puncture in the bag, even with the point of a needle, the instrument would be spoiled, and the bag would immediately collapse; and this is frequently done by humorous people, when they wish to irritate the pipers. It is evident that this instrument must be a very good incentive to their courage at the time of battle, for by its tones, the Irish are stirred up to fight in the same manner as the soldiers of other nations by the trumpet."

From the statement of Galilei, it would also appear to have been used as an accompaniment to the *caionan* at funerals, in the sixteenth century. "It is much used (he says, in a passage respecting the bagpipe) by the Irish; to its sound this unconquered, fierce, and warlike people march their armies, and encourage each other to deeds of valour. With it also they accompany their dead to the grave, making such mournful sounds as to invite, nay almost force the bystanders to weep."

That the bagpipe was also our proper military musical instrument in the fifteenth century appears from the account of those Irish who accompanied the army of King Edward to Calais, under the leading of the Prior of Kilmainham;[a] and we now proceed to give a specimen of the same instrument, as known to the Irish about A. D. 1300. This ludicrous but curious illustration is from a manuscript of the *Dinnseanchus*, a collection of Irish history and topography, executed, according to Doctor O'Connor, about the above year.[b] It forms part of an initial letter at the commencement of one of the chapters, and represents a

[a] Smith's Hist. Cork, vol. ii. p. 43.

[b] Rer. Hib. Script. Vet. vol. i. Proleg. 175.

pig gravely occupied in performing on the pipes, much in the same mode as in the foregoing example.

He presses the bag against his belly with the foreleg,

> And from his lungs into the bag is blown
> Supply of needful air to feed the growling drone,

which appears double, and ornamented with encircling straps, probably of brass. Four holes are represented open on the chanter, but whether the whole number intended be five or six, it is difficult to say. Certainly the instrument is not so complete as that of the Elizabethan period, but it is unquestionable that it had been known from time immemorial among the Irish, for in all the remaining poems descriptive of the Teach-Midchuarta, varying in date from the tenth to the sixth century, constant mention is made of the *cushlannaig* or bag-pipes.[a] The antiquity, therefore, of our old airs of the defective class can as little be impeached, on the ground of our not having had the bagpipe in early times, as can that of the more florid class on a similar objection to the antiquity of the harp.

The bagpipe still flourishes among us; but, as the harp is now irretrievably gone, it seems a duty to our national instrument to conclude the history of its decline and fall by adding an account of the various efforts made for its revival, as well as some notices of the last of that race of minstrels, composers, and musicians, whose performance on it has given Ireland one of the strongest claims she has yet asserted for a place of distinction at the board of nations.

[a] Petrie on the Antiquities of Tara Hill, Trans. R. I. A., vol. xviii.

CHAPTER IV.

OF THE VARIOUS EFFORTS TO REVIVE THE IRISH HARP.

Of the estimation in which performers on this noble instrument were once held in Ireland it would be superfluous here to speak. Mr. Walker, in his history of the Irish Bards, has given an account of their power and privileges in former times, of the efforts made for their suppression, as persons dangerous to the State at a later period, and of their reduced condition in his own day. The latter chapters of his work may, indeed, justly be entitled a history of "The Decline and Fall of the Irish Harp." Yet, before it finally sunk into its present total disuse, there were some efforts, worthy of better success, but hitherto unrecorded, made for its revival. After the death of Carolan, and the subsidence of that enthusiasm which his charming compositions had produced, the condition of the harpers had gradually declined. Persons of the better class had not for a length of time adopted native music as a profession, and, among the numerous wandering performers whom Carolan's success had called into the field, there were, no doubt, many whose conduct reflected little credit on their calling. Still the representatives of the genuine old school had not altogether disappeared from the tables and entertainments of the gentry of native Irish family. Of the latter class was Arthur O'Neill, whose manners and acquirements were such as at that period would not have been inconsistent with the pretensions of many country gentlemen. The following letter from Doctor M'Donnell, who was taught, when a youth, to play on the harp by O'Neill, will be found to contain not only a just tribute to the worthy minstrel's character, but a very faithful account of the general condition of our harpers at the period referred to.

"Belfast, *November 8th*, 1838.

"My dear Mr. Bunting,

"In compliance with your request, I furnish you with some particulars of my acquaintance with Arthur O'Neill, the Irish harper, from whom you procured some information prior to your first publication. My father, who had a great fondness for music, selected O'Neill as the most proper person he then knew to teach his children, and he lived in our house for two years in this capacity; but my father's death, in 1780, put an end to this study, which we found very difficult, on account of the teacher being blind. At that period almost all harpers were blind, this profession having been humanely reserved as a provision for the sons of reduced gentlemen who happened to be blind, a calamity then much more common than at present, owing to improvements in the treatment of small-pox. During the two years he lived in the house, he was treated as a poor gentleman, and had a servant. He was a man of strong natural sense, pleasing in his manners, and had acquired a considerable knowledge of the common topics, so that he could acquit himself very well in mixed society, when encouraged to converse. He had, according to the custom of these itinerant musicians, travelled several times over all Ireland, and became thereby acquainted with several of the principal families, who were in the habit of entertaining such persons; among these there were some Protestant families, but the harpers frequented mostly the houses of old Irish families, who had lost their titles, or were reduced more or less in their estates. These they would visit once in two or three years, and remain from a week to a month in each house; and it was generally a day of rejoicing among the young and the old when one of those itinerants appeared. As to the character of O'Neill, I found him a perfectly safe companion, a man of veracity and integrity, not at all addicted to boasting or pretending to any thing extraordinary; he never affected to compose or alter any tune, but played it exactly as he had been taught by his master Hugh O'Neill, for whom he always expressed great veneration.

"I think, therefore, you may rely with the greatest confidence upon any information he gave you as to the technical names of the strings and parts of the harp, and names of the different notes, or strokes upon the harp. He was as incapable, as he would have been disinclined, to have invented these terms, which I think of great consequence, as connected with the literary history of music: and if in the course of human events, your singular ingenuity, zeal, and success, in discovering those ancient airs, shall be the means of preserving O'Neill's name also from oblivion, it will always gratify me to remember that I was the means of introducing you to each other.

"And I am, dear Bunting, most sincerely yours,

"J. M'Donnell."

Incited by the benevolent and patriotic desire of elevating the condition of this harmless race of men, and of restoring our native music to its due place in public estimation, Mr. James Dungan, an Irish gentleman, resident in Copenhagen, conceived the idea of instituting annual meetings, where skill in the composition and performance of native airs should be encouraged by liberal premiums, and in which the gentry of the country might be induced to take an interest, by making each meeting the occasion of a splendid ball. For this purpose he remitted sufficient funds, and, although not in the country himself, succeeded in A. D. 1781, in bringing about the first meeting for the revival of our national music at his native town, Granard, in the county of Longford. The harpers present were Charles Fanning, Patrick Kerr, Patrick Maguire, Hugh Higgins, Charles Berreen, Rose Mooney, and O'Neill, from whom we have the following characteristic account of the meeting. "Charles Fanning got the first premium, ten guineas, for 'The Coolin;' I got the second, eight guineas, for the 'Greenwoods of Truagh' and 'Mrs. Crofton;' and Rose Mooney got the third, five guineas, for 'Planxty Burke.' The judges at the first ball were excellent, and there was some difficulty in deciding the first premium between Fanning and me; but in consequence of my endeavouring to appear on this occasion *in my very best*, they decided in favour of Charles, who was careless in his dress, saying at the same time that he wanted money more than I did: however, I received many handsome verbal compliments. To the best of my opinion, there were at least 500 persons at the ball, which was held in the Market-house. A Mr. Burrowes was one of the stewards; he was a tolerable judge of music, and was so angry at the decision of the premiums, *that he thrust his cane through one of the windows*."[a]

The second ball, which was held on the 2nd of March, in the succeeding year, was still better and more numerously attended than the first; but the decay of the harp at this time appears strongly from the fact, that, notwithstanding the celebrity of the first meeting, two new candidates were all that presented themselves in addition to those already enumerated. The names of the new comers were Edward M'Dermott Roe, and Catherine Martin. The premiums were adjudged as before. Mr. Dungan himself came from Copenhagen, to be present at the last ball, which was, in consequence, the most splendid of the three. The only new names in the list of harpers on this occasion were, Laurence Keane and James Duncan. Unfortunately, the meeting appears to have been marred by private jealousies, which had so disheartening an effect on the munificent originator and patron, that he did not afterwards attempt the renewal of these interesting assemblies.

O'Neill, with his usual simplicity and quaintness, thus describes the last harpers' ball at Granard: "A gentleman, named Miles Keane, railed uncommonly about the distribution of the premiums, (they were adjudged as at the first and second meetings,) and swore a great oath, 'That it was the most *nefarious* decision he ever witnessed.' I don't know what he meant, but he used the expression. Lord and Lady Longford attended this ball, and the meeting was vastly more numerous than at either of the two former ones. Quality [persons of rank] forty miles round attended, and there was not a house in the town but was filled with ladies and gentlemen, and the town was like a horse fair, as there was not stabling for the twentieth part of the horses that came; there were at least 1000 people at the ball. In consequence of the harpers who obtained no premiums having been neglected on the former occasions, I hinted a subscription, which was well received, and performed; and indeed, on distributing the collection, their proportions exceeded our premiums."

Ten years afterwards, the spirit which had animated Mr. Dungan spread itself northward. Some gentlemen of Belfast and its neighbourhood (among others, Doctor M'Donnell, the late Robert Bradshaw, and Henry Joy, Esqrs., were the most active,) resolved on imitating the example of their patriotic countryman, and for that purpose issued the following notification:

"BELFAST, *December*, 1791.

"Some inhabitants of Belfast, feeling themselves interested in every thing which relates to the honour, as well as the prosperity of their country, propose to open a subscription,

[a] MS. autobiography of O'Neill *penes* the Editor.

which they intend to apply in attempting to revive and perpetuate *the ancient music and poetry of Ireland.* They are solicitous to preserve from oblivion the few fragments which have been permitted to remain as monuments of the refined taste and genius of their ancestors.

"In order to carry this project into execution, it must appear obvious to those acquainted with the situation of this country that it will be necessary to assemble the *harpers*, those descendants of our ancient bards, who are at present almost exclusively possessed of all that remains of the *music*, *poetry*, and *oral traditions of Ireland.*

"It is proposed, that the harpers should be induced to assemble at Belfast, (suppose on the 1st of July next,) by the distribution of such prizes as may seem adequate to the subscribers; and that a person well versed in the language and antiquities of this nation should attend, with a skilful musician to transcribe and arrange the most beautiful and interesting parts of their knowledge.

"An undertaking of this nature will, undoubtedly, meet the approbation of men of refinement and erudition in every country. And when it is considered how intimately the *spirit* and *character* of a *people* are connected with their *national poetry* and *music*, it is presumed that the Irish patriot and politician will not deem it an object unworthy his patronage and protection."

Ten harpers only responded to this call, a sufficient proof of the declining state of the art, and of the necessity which now manifestly existed of noting down as many as possible of those musical treasures which might so soon perish along with their venerable repositories. This was the office assigned to the Editor, and in discharging it, he first imbibed that passion for Irish melody which has never ceased to animate him since. It was well that the security of notation was so soon resorted to, for, even in 1809, at the time of the Editor's second publication, two only of the ten harpers assembled at Belfast on this occasion were surviving, and these two are long since dead. The meeting was held in the large room of the Exchange at Belfast, on the 11th, 12th, and 13th July, 1792, and was attended by :

Denis Hempson, (blind,) from the county of Derry, aged 97 years, (but there is reason to believe he was older by several years,—see his memoir,) played "The dawning of the day;" "Ull a condo wo," or "The county of Leitrim." Authors and dates unknown.

Arthur O'Neill, (blind,) from the county of Tyrone, aged 58 years, played "Green woods of Truagh," author and date unknown, and "Mrs. Crofton," by Carolan.

Charles Fanning, from the county of Cavan, aged 56, played "Car a Ceann dilis," or "Black-headed deary," author and date unknown; "Rose Dillon," and "Jig," (Carolan;) "Colonel O'Hara," (Carolan.)

Daniel Black, (blind,) from the county of Derry, aged 75, played "The receipt for drinking whiskey," (Carolan;) "Sir Festus a Burke," and "Thomas a Burke," (Carolan.)

Charles Byrne, from the county of Leitrim, aged 80, played "The old Truagha," author and date unknown; "Oganioge," very ancient; author and date unknown.

HUGH HIGGINS, (blind,) from the county of Mayo, aged 55, played "Slieve Gallen," ancient, and "Madam Cole," (Carolan.)

PATRICK QUIN, (blind,) from the county of Armagh, aged 47, played "The rocks of pleasure," ancient; "Carolan's devotion," and "Grace Nugent," (Carolan.)

WILLIAM CARR, from the county of Armagh, aged 15, played "The dawning of the day," ancient.

ROSE MOONEY, (blind,) from the county of Meath, aged 52, played "Sir Charles Coote," "Mrs. Judge," and "Mrs. French," or "Fanny Power," all by Carolan.

JAMES DUNCAN, from the county of Down, aged 45, played "Molly Bheag O," author and date unknown; "Morning star," and "Catherine Tyrrell," ancient.

Besides the tunes annexed to the names of the performers, the following were played, forming a portion of those airs held in the greatest esteem by the harpers:

"Molly Bheagh O," or "Little Molly O." Ancient.
"Miss Moore," or "The Hawk of Ballyshannon," O'Cahan.
"Planxty Kingsland," . . . . Carolan.
"Graga-nish," or "Love in secret," . . T. Conallon.
"Denis Daly," . . . . Carolan.
"Fanny Power," . . . . Do.
"Collough an Tinnic," or "The sleeping Fox," Ancient.
"Coolin," . . . . Do.
"Carolan's Concerto," . . . . . . Carolan.
"Lady Letitia Burke," . . . . Do.
"Bacach buidhe na leimne," "The lame yellow beggar." O'Cahan.
"Scara na Gumbanagh," "The parting of friends." Ancient.
"Cathal Mhac Aodha," "Charles M'Hugh," Very ancient.
"Mable Kelly," . . . . Carolan.
"Lady Iveagh," . . . . T. Conallon.
"Tiarna Mayo," "Lord Mayo," . . Murphy.
"Eibhlin a Ruin," "Ellen a Roon," . Ancient.
"Maidin bheag aoibhinn," "Soft mild morning." Ancient.
"Nancy Cooper," . . . . Carolan.
"Carolan's Cap," . . . . Do.
"Lady Blaney," . . . . Do.
"Mrs. Maxwell," . . . . Do.
"Pleararca na Ruarc," or "O'Rourke's feast." Carolan.
"Doctor Hart," . . . . Do.
"Carrick an evenish," or "Pleasant Rocks," Ancient.
"Sheela na Conallon," . . . . T. Conallon.
"Sir Festus a Burke," . . . . Carolan.
"The humours of Whiskey,"[a] . . . Do.
"Cathleen Tyrrell," . . . . Ancient.

The Irish harpers were succeeded by a Welshman,[b] whose execution was very great; the contrast between the sweet, expressive tones of the Irish instrument, and the bold, martial ones of the Welsh, had a pleasing effect, as marking the difference of character between the two nations.

On the following day, the highest premium, ten guineas, was adjudged to Fanning;[c] eight guineas to Arthur O'Neill; and six to each of the others.

[a] The same as Carolan's Receipt.

[b] The Welsh harper's name was *Williams;* he was a good performer, and died on ship board soon after this date.

[c] Fanning was not the best performer, but he succeeded in getting the first prize, by playing "The Coolin," with modern variations; a piece of music at that time much in request by young practitioners on the piano forte.

The fund for remunerating the harpers was raised by subscription, and by tickets for admission during the three days of performance, at half a guinea each; and the meetings were attended by all the nobility and chief gentry of the district.

When the proceedings were terminated, all the harpers were invited to dinner by Doctor Macdonnell; "And if we had all been peers of the realm," says O'Neill, "we could not have been better treated; the assiduity of the Doctor and his family, to make us happy, was more than I can describe."

It may be interesting to the reader to know something of the personal appearance of these last representatives of a class so famous in song and history. They were in general clad in a comfortable homely manner, in drab-coloured or grey cloth, of coarse manufacture. A few of them made an attempt at splendour, by wearing silver buttons on their coats, particularly Higgins and O'Neill; the former had his buttons decorated with his initials only, but O'Neill had his initials, surmounted by the crest of the O'Neills, engraved on silver buttons the size of half a crown. Some had horses and guides when travelling through the country; others their attendants only, who carried their harps. They seemed perfectly happy and contented with their lot, and all appeared convinced of the excellence of the genuine *old Irish music*, which they said had existed for centuries, and, from its delightful melody, would continue to exist for centuries to come. The Editor well remembers the anguish with which O'Neill contemplated the extinction of the old strains, which he said had been the delight of the Irish nation for so many years; he called them, with tears coursing down his aged cheeks, "*The dear! dear! sweet old Irish tunes.*"

The *third* attempt at reviving our music, was the formation of the *Belfast Irish Harp Society*, instituted for the support of a teacher, and the tuition of a number of boys, from the age of ten years, among the blind and indigent, who were supplied with lodging and board. It was conducted with much zeal at its commencement, in 1807; and it terminated, in consequence of a decline of pecuniary supplies, in 1813.

From that time Arthur O'Neill, the blind teacher, was paid an annuity of £30 till his death, by a few members of the society, in consideration of his abilities and good conduct in the school. The affairs of the society were under the government of a committee, treasurer, and secretary, yearly chosen by the members at large. For some years the number of subscribers fluctuated between 100 and 120, the greatest sum paid in one year being £150. During the six years of its existence, the expenditure, amounted to £950.

This society had the credit of preserving the Irish harp from being, perhaps, for ever lost; as it appears that, six years afterwards, the new society, instituted in 1819 by the bounty of friends in India, discovered no harpers in Ireland, save those who derived their education from Arthur O'Neill, master in the first school.

About the time of the first Belfast Society, a Harp Association was founded in Dublin, and a considerable fund collected for it, but it did not succeed.

The *fourth* effort to rescue our national instrument from ruin, was, strangely enough, made by residents in India.[a] At their head, as an honorary member, was our illustrious countryman, the late Marquis of Hastings, then Governor-General in India, and a liberal contributor to the fund; also the Marquis of Downshire, the Marquis of Donegall, and the Earl of Belfast, as honorary members, resident in Ireland.

The contributors in India consisted of a number of spirited noblemen and gentlemen,[b] generally natives of Ireland, by whom remittances were made to a large amount, exceeding £1100. The school appeared to flourish for a few years under the superintendance of Rainey, a nephew of the Scotch poet, Burns, who had been educated in the school of the former society, under O'Neill, and became a very good harper; but since his death, the affairs of the society have been in a declining state, and the following copy of a letter to the Editor, from the secretary, will shew that it is now nearly extinct, with little prospect of its ever being revived.

"DONEGALL-STREET, *30th July*, 1839.

"DEAR SIR,

"In answer to your inquiries respecting the Harp Society, I am sorry to inform you that the funds will be exhausted about the first of February next. After the first of August, we shall have only two boys; we are anxious to prolong the time, that one of the boys (William Murphy) may have as much instruction as can be afforded, he having his eyesight perfect, and a natural taste for music. We were most desirous to have one Irish harper who could read music, and thereby keep alive, for some time longer, a number of those national airs which, so far as the Irish harp is concerned, were about to be lost for ever. I mentioned to you that we might probably keep up the society for a few years longer by private subscription, but from the fact that the young harpers can only earn their bread by

[a] Odd as it may appear, a warm admirer of Irish music was found in those remote parts, in the late *King of Oude*. This potentate had contracted a partiality for our harp and music, from the resemblance they bore to the music and to some of the instruments of his own country, which were, like the Irish harp, strung with wire. In consequence, he caused application to be made through the late John Williamson Fulton, Esq., of Lisburn, (then a principal of the mercantile house of Macintosh and Co., at Calcutta,) to the Editor, at that time one of the managers of the Harp Society at Belfast, requesting that the society would send him a harper and piper, for whom he purposed to make a splendid provision. The society were unwilling to part with Rainey, then master of the school, and there was no other harper who could be deemed sufficiently master of his instrument to support the musical pretensions of the country with credit at a foreign court. However, not to treat his Highness's commands with disrespect, the society forwarded him a very good piper, provided with an excellent pair of Irish union bag-pipes. This piper was honourably received, and much caressed at Calcutta, but having addicted himself to *arrack*, he lost his opportunities, and never reached his destination. The story goes, that he was drowned in the Ganges, having fallen off the forecastle of the pleasure barge sent to convey him to his Highness's residence, while performing on the pipes. It is farther said, that the tune he was playing, when he fell over board, was "Carolan's Receipt;" but this, probably, is an invention.

[b] Among these may be enumerated, the Marquis of Hastings, General Sir William Casement, Sir Francis M'Naghten, Major Charles Kennedy and his brothers, John Williamson Fulton, Esq., A. Gordon Caulfield, Esq., &c. &c.

playing in hotels, where they are too liable to contract fatal habits, we think the money could be more usefully laid out in other charities. Our gentry in Ireland are too scarce, and too little national, to encourage itinerant harpers, as of old ; besides, the taste and fashion of music no longer bears upon our national instrument : it had its day, but, like all other fashions, it must give way to novelty.

"Truly yours,

"JOHN M'ADAM.

"*Edw. Bunting, Esq.*"

CHAPTER V.

ANECDOTES OF THE MORE DISTINGUISHED HARPERS OF THE LAST TWO CENTURIES.

THE aspect of society in Ireland during the seventeenth and eighteenth centuries exhibits some very peculiar and interesting features. The same disposition to adopt native manners, which had formerly obtained for the great Anglo-Norman families the character of being *Hibernicis ipsis Hiberniores*, now shewed itself, though in a greatly modified degree, among the new residents introduced by the plantation of Ulster, and the other important changes which took place subsequent to that event. And, as the Burkes, Butlers, and Fitzgeralds, of the feudal period, were always found to become more Irish in proportion as their power was less disputed, so the Cuffes, Cootes, Kings, and other noble families of the latter epoch, began almost immediately, on the first establishment of their ascendancy, to blend the manners of the two countries, infusing more or less of Irishism into the mixture as the fortunes of their party appeared more or less predominant. It is to this epoch we are to look back for the formation of that fine and interesting character, the Irish gentleman of the old school ; a character which, unfortunately, we can now only contemplate in the retrospect ; for, ever since the commencement of the political disputes which have embroiled the latter end of the last, and all that has yet elapsed of the present, century, our nobility and gentry have been gradually conforming again to the English model, a change, no doubt, in many respects desirable and expedient, but one which has, alas ! brought about the utter ruin of the Irish harp.

In the following notices of the harpers who have flourished during this period, any information minute enough to be interesting is chiefly confined to the latter end of the last century, when the abandonment of Irish manners had already begun ; yet even the passing glimpses of society in Ireland, as it was from sixty to a hundred years since, which these anecdotes afford, give what it is hoped will be found an amusing, if not instructive, insight into the habits and tastes of certainly the most warm-hearted, and the most grotesquely, and at the same time pathetically, humorous people on the face of the earth.

Rory Dall O'Cahan, already alluded to as being manifestly the Rory Dall Morison of Scottish tradition, may be taken as the first of these our later harpers, both in point of date and celebrity. He is remembered to this day throughout the North of Ireland as one of the chief O'Cahans, of the O'Cahan country; and the names of the estates to which he is supposed to have been entitled were still enumerated in tradition at the time of the meeting of the harpers at Belfast. Being blind, (whether from his youth or birth does not appear,) he early devoted himself to the harp, but, as may be surmised, not with a view to music as a profession; for the tradition invariably preserved of him in Antrim and Derry is, that he travelled into Scotland shortly before the accession of King James the Sixth of that country to the throne of England, attended by the retinue of a gentleman of figure; and when in Scotland, according to the accounts preserved there also, he seemed to have travelled in the company of noble persons.[a]

Among other visits made by him to the houses of the Scottish nobility, he is said to have called at Eglintoun Castle, now celebrated in the annals of modern chivalry, when Lady Eglintoun, not being aware of his rank, affronted his Irish pride by demanding a tune in a peremptory manner. O'Cahan refused, and left the castle. Her ladyship afterwards, understanding who he was, sought a reconciliation, which was readily effected. This incident gave occasion to the composition, by O'Cahan, of the appropriate tune of "Da mihi manum," or "Give me your hand,"[b] the fame of which afterwards spread throughout Scotland, and reaching the ear of the king, induced him to send for the composer. O'Cahan accordingly attended at the Scottish court, and so delighted the royal circle with his performance, that James walked towards him, and laid his hand familiarly on his shoulder. One of the courtiers present remarking on the honour thus conferred on him, Rory observed, "A greater than King James has laid his hand on my shoulder." "Who was that, man!" cried the king. "O'Neil, Sire,"—replied Rory, standing up. Such, at least, were the tales preserved of him among the Irish harpers fifty years since; and, making all allowances for national vanity and exaggeration, he must be regarded as having been a man of considerable consequence and great ability. He was the composer of the famous airs of Port Atholl, Port Gordon, Port Lennox, Lude's Supper, Da Mihi Manum, &c. &c., the first and last of which are given in the present collection. Sir Walter Scott, with his usual skill in employing facts for the illustration of his tales, introduces the name of Rory Dall as "the most famous harper of the Western Highlands" in his legend of Montrose, where he makes him the instructor of Annot Lyle. It is certain that he died in Scotland, at the house of a person of distinction, where he left his harp and silver tuning-key, and that during the latter part of his career he was reduced to very indigent circumstances. The foregoing account is given chiefly on the authority of Arthur O'Neill and Hempson.

[a] Gunn's Essay, p. 95.

[b] Known in Ireland as "Tabhair dom lamh."

Cotemporary with O'Cahan were JOHN and HARRY SCOTT, two brothers, born in the county of Westmeath, both eminent composers and performers. They were particularly distinguished for their *caoinans* or dirge pieces. In this line they have produced pathetic movements for Purcell, Baron of Loughmoe, and O'Hussey, Baron of Galtrim, respectively.

About this time, also, lived GERALD O'DALY, the reputed composer of *Aileen a Roon*, though, from the marks of high antiquity apparent throughout the air, it is probable that he only adapted the Irish words to it. O'Daly is said to have been a man of rank and learning, and cultivated music only as an accomplishment.

Another eminent harper of this period was MILES REILLY, of Killincarra, in the county of Cavan, born about 1635. He was universally referred to by the harpers at Belfast as the composer of the original "Lochabar.' This air is supposed to have been carried into Scotland by THOMAS CONNALLON, born five years later at Cloonmahon, in the county of Sligo. O'Neill calls him "the great harper," and states that he attained to city honors ("they made him, as I heard, a 'baillie,' or kind of Burgomaster"[a]) in Edinburgh, where he died. His celebrity in Ireland was very great, as may be judged of from the following elegant ode, which has been preserved by Mr. Hardiman, and is thus translated :

I.

Enchanter, who reignest
  Supreme o'er the North,
Who hast wiled the coy spirit
  Of true music forth ;
In vain Europe's minstrels
  To honour aspire,
When thy swift, slender fingers
  Go forth on the wire !

II.

There is no heart's desire
  Can be felt by a king,
That thy hand cannot snatch
  From the soul of the string ;
By the magical virtue
  And might of its sway ;
For, charmer, thou stealest
  Thy notes from a fay !

III.

Enchanter, I say ;
  For thy magical skill
Can soothe every sorrow,
  And heal every ill ;
Who hear thee, they praise thee,
  And weep while they praise,
For charmer, thou stealest
  Thy strain from the fays !

Such complimentary addresses were at this time usual, and the praises bestowed by the anonymous poet on O'Connallon are in no way more liberal than those lavished on THADDEUS O'COFFEY, another performer of the same epoch, by the learned Keating in an ode already cited.

[a] O'Neill's MS.

O'Connallon was the composer of "The dawning of the day" or "The Golden Star," "Love in secret," "Bonny Jean," "The Jointure," "Molly St. George," &c., as well as of a vast number of airs now lost. His brother WILLIAM O'CONNALLON, born about 1645, affected a different style, in which, however, he produced pieces of high merit; among these may be enumerated "Lady Iveagh," "Saely Kelly," "Molly M'Alpine," &c. &c.

We have now arrived among the immediate cotemporaries of Carolan, of whom MURPHY, a Leinster man, was always spoken of by O'Neill as having borne a higher reputation as a performer than any other harper who had been heard by his (O'Neill's) contemporaries. Murphy had travelled into France, and played with approbation before Louis le Grand; but on his return to this country, his assumed airs and ostentatious finery procured him much dislike, especially from Carolan, who on one occasion nearly beat him to death in a tavern, at Castleblaney. The air "Lord Mayo" has been attributed to him; though the words of this truly characteristic and touching song, as given by Mr. Hardiman, would seem strongly to confirm Mr. O'Connor's statement of the piece having been composed, at a much earlier period, by David Murphy, a native of Connaught, and a retainer of the nobleman whose anger it deprecates.

CORNELIUS LYONS, harper to the Earl of Antrim, was another of Carolan's cotemporaries; but he was also his companion in friendship, as well as his rival in art, even as a composer. Only one of his melodies is preserved, called "Miss Hamilton," but his variations to the tunes of "Ellen a Roon," "Callenagh a voch a thoo Sharsha," (Girls, did you see George,) called also "Connor Macarcavy;" "Green sleeves," "The Coolan," and several others, evince a very graceful and elegant genius. He was, besides, a person of good manners and attainments, and Lord Antrim himself took much pleasure in his conversation. O'Neill relates the following adventure of our harper and his patron in London: "His lordship was both a wit and a poet, and delighted in equality, where vulgarity was not too gross. At one time, he and Lyons, when in London, went to the house of a famous Irish harper, named Heffernan, who kept a tavern there; but, before hand, they formed the following plan. 'I will call you Cousin Burke,' said his lordship. 'You may call me either Cousin Randall or My Lord, as you please.' After regaling for some time, Heffernan was called up, who was, by this time, well aware of the dignity of his guest from the conversation and livery of his lordship's servants. When Heffernan came into the room, he was desired to bring in his harp and sit down, which he did, and played a good many tunes in a grand style. His lordship then called upon his cousin Burke to play a tune. The supposed cousin, after many apologies, at length took the harp, and played some of his best airs. Heffernan, after listening a little while, started up and exclaimed, 'My lord, you may call him Cousin Burke, or what cousin you please, but, *dar dieh*, he plays upon Lyons's fingers.' What is very extraordinary, Heffernan had never seen Lyons before."[a] His lordship then retired, leaving the minstrels to indulge in Bacchanalian rivalry, which O'Neill assures us they did "like bards of old."

[a] The O'Neill MS.

Of CAROLAN himself so much has been written, that comparatively little remains to be done here, either in illustrating the fertility of his genius, or in recounting the whimsical adventures and practical jokes for which his memory is famous. He was born in the year 1670, at Nobber, or, as some assert, at a neighbouring village, in the county of Westmeath, and died at the age of 68, in the year 1738. Early deprived of his sight by the small-pox, the inhabitant of a country recently desolated by a civil war, and, add to these his propensity to dissipation, we must wonder at the proofs he has given of the depth and versatility of his talents. Some idea of the fertility of his invention may be formed from this circumstance, that *one* harper who attended the Belfast meeting in 1792, and who had never seen Carolan, nor been taught by any person who had an opportunity of imitating him, had acquired upwards of one hundred of his tunes, which, he asserted, constituted but an inconsiderable portion of them. As an instance of the facility with which he committed tunes to memory, as well as of the astonishing ease with which he could produce new melodies, take the following fact, vouched for by the *Monthly Review*.[a] " At the house of an Irish nobleman, where Geminiani was present, Carolan challenged that eminent composer to a trial of skill. The musician played over on his violin the fifth concerto of Vivaldi. It was instantly repeated by Carolan on his harp, although he had never heard it before. The surprise of the company was increased when he asserted that he would compose a concerto himself at the moment; and the more so, when he actually played that admirable piece known ever since as Carolan's Concerto." He composed, as one who knew him well reported, upon the buttons of his coat, taking them as representatives of the lines and spaces; as Stanley, the blind organist, used to compose on a slate with convex lines. Carolan was the first who departed from the purely Irish style in composition; but, although he delighted in the polished compositions of the Italian and German school, with which style many of his airs are strongly tinctured, yet he felt the full excellence of the ancient music of his own country, and has been heard to say that he would rather have been the author of Molly M'Alpine,[b] (a charming original air, by O'Connallon,) than of any melody he himself had ever composed. Yet it must be admitted that he has produced some airs of surpassing tenderness, and of purely Irish structure. Such, for instance, is his sweet and touching "Bridget Cruise,"[c] addressed to a lady to whom he was tenderly but hopelessly attached. It is the only one remaining of fifteen different pieces addressed by him to this lady. In connexion with this delightful strain, the reader will, of course, bear in mind the well known anecdote of Carolan, when on a pilgrimage at Loch Derg, recognizing the object of his youthful affections by the touch of her hand, in assisting her out of the ferry boat. His arrangement of the "Fairy Queen,"[d] is another of these admirable realizations of the true old idea of national melody. In the same class may be enumerated "Rose Dillon,"[e] and his "Receipt for Drinking," the last,

[a] Old Series, vol. lxxvii.

[b] [c] [d] [e] These airs will all be found in the Editor's former collection.

however, inspired by a much less amiable predilection than any of the others, yet still infinitely sweet, lively, and harmonious.

So many anecdotes have been related of Carolan, of his follies and foibles, and the good-humoured jokes played upon him by his associates, that it is unnecessary to heighten a picture already drawn in vivid colours. One anecdote only of this sort appears worth adding, as from the circumstantial nature of its details it effectually negatives the possibility of "Bumper Squire Jones," which has recently been claimed as an English tune, being other than the legitimate and spontaneous offspring of Carolan's own genius. The story is given on the authority of O'Neill, who dictated it to the writer of his MS. Memoirs, at least forty years ago. Carolan, when he came to the county of Antrim, used to resort to Moneyglass, the residence of Thomas Morris Jones, Esq. When he was composing the music of that celebrated song, the paraphrase of which, by Baron Dawson, has immortalized the "Bumper Squire," he was overheard by one Moore, the keeper of a tavern in the town of Antrim, where he put up. Moore had a ready ear for music and played tolerably on the violin, so that when Carolan, after completing his inimitable piece, came to him, boasting that he had now struck out a melody which he was sure would please the Squire, Moore was prepared not only to insist, like our English cotemporary, that the air was an old and common one, but actually to play it note for note upon the violin. This of course threw Carolan into an ungovernable fury. However, when his passion had spent itself, an explanation took place, and a drinking bout, the usual termination of such scenes, concluded the affair. When at Castle Archdall too,[a] a similar trick was played upon him by Lyons, who stole his tune of "Mrs. Archdall," during its composition, and to enhance his annoyance, assumed the character of one Berreen, a strolling harper of mean abilities, the very mention of whose name was enough to excite Carolan's bile. To render the deception more complete, Lyons got a humorous fellow, called M'Dermott, to mimic Berreen's voice while he played "Mrs. Archdall" in the most wretched style on his harp. So great was Carolan's rage, that he protested he would never enter the door of Castle Archdall again, if Berreen were not immediately put in the stocks. To the stocks accordingly they dragged, or pretended to drag M'Dermott, and the deception was continued until Carolan himself made the wag fain to resume his natural voice by belabouring him with his cane where he sat.

A miniature representation of the bard is prefixed, taken from a portrait now in the possession of Sir Henry Marsh, Baronet. The features are graceful and pleasing, and the expression that of rapt attention to the melody which he draws from the harp.

He lies buried at Kilronan, in the county of Westmeath, where his skull was formerly preserved in a niche, like that of Grace O'Malley, at Clare Island. He was unquestionably a great genius, both as a composer and a poet; but it is equally certain that he never excelled as a performer: this may be attributed to the fact, that he did not begin to learn the harp till

[a] When Charles O'Connor once asked Carolan, if he had been to visit Mr. Archdall? "No," replied Carolan, "but I have been to visit a prince."—(*Walker.*)

he was upwards of sixteen, at which age the fingers have lost the suppleness that must be taken advantage of in early years, to produce a really master hand.

DENIS A HAMPSY or HEMPSON, with whom the Editor of this collection was many years ago struck as a model of the old Irish school, was born shortly after Carolan, in the year 1695. He had been in Carolan's company when a youth, but never took pleasure in playing his compositions. The pieces which he delighted to perform were unmixed with modern refinements, which he seemed studiously to avoid; confining himself chiefly to the most antiquated of those strains which have long survived the memory of their composers, and even a knowledge of the ages that produced them. Hempson was the only one of the harpers at the Belfast Meeting, in 1792, who literally played the harp with long crooked nails, as described by the old writers. In playing, he caught the string between the flesh and the nail; not like the other harpers of his day, who pulled it by the fleshy part of the finger alone. He had an admirable method of playing *Staccato* and *Legato,* in which he could run through rapid divisions in an astonishing style. His fingers lay over the strings in such a manner, that when he struck them with one finger, the other was instantly ready to stop the vibration, so that the Staccato passages were heard in full perfection. When asked the reason of his playing certain parts of the tune or lesson in that style, his reply was, "That is the way I learned it," or "I cannot play it in any other." The intricacy and peculiarity of his playing often amazed the Editor, who could not avoid perceiving in it vestiges of a noble system of practice, that had existed for many centuries; strengthening the opinion, that the Irish were, at a very early period, superior to the other nations of Europe, both in the composition and performance of music. In fact, Hempson's Staccato and Legato passages, double slurs, shakes, turns, graces, &c. &c., comprised as great a range of execution as has ever been devised by the most modern improvers.[a]

An accurate portrait of Hempson, when above one hundred years old, was inserted in the Editor's former collection, and is given here in miniature. The following account of him, communicated in a letter from the late Rev. George Sampson, the historian of Londonderry, was originally published by Miss Owenson, now Lady Morgan, in her admired novel, "The Wild Irish Girl." Were the writer still alive, the Editor is satisfied he would approve of his memoir being transplanted into a work to which it is so peculiarly suited, and where it will be handed down with the minstrel's favourite music.

"*July 3rd,* 1805.

"I made the survey of the man with two heads, [in allusion to an enormous excrescence

[a] The late Mr. Seybold, the celebrated performer on the Pedal Harp, being in a gentleman's house in Belfast, in 1800, when Arthur O'Neill was present, declared his admiration of the old man's shake on the Irish harp, which was performed apparently with the greatest ease and execution; admitting that he could not do it himself in the same manner on his own instrument, the shake being of the greatest difficulty on every species of harp.

or wen on the back of his head,] according to your desire, but not till yesterday, on account of various impossibilities; here is my report:

"Denis Hempson, or the man with two heads, is a native of Craigmore, near Garvagh, in the county of Londonderry. His father, Bryan Darragher (blackish complexion) Hempson, held the whole townland of Tyrcrevan; his mother's relations were in possession of the Woodtown, (both considerable farms at Magilligan.) He lost his sight at the age of three years by the small-pox; at twelve years old he began to learn the harp under Bridget O'Cahan; 'for,' as he said, 'in these old times, *women* as well as men were taught the Irish harp in the best families, and every old Irish family had harps in plenty.' His next instructor was John C. Garragher, a blind travelling harper, whom he followed to Buncranagh, where his master used to play for Colonel Vaughan; he had afterwards Loughlin Fanning and Patrick Connor, in succession, as masters. 'All these were from Connaught, which was,' as he added, 'the best part of the kingdom for Irish harpers, and for music.' At eighteen years of age he began to play for himself, and was taken into the house of Counsellor Canning, at Garvagh, for half a year; his host, with Squire Gage and Doctor Bacon, joined, and bought him a harp.

"He travelled nine or ten years through Ireland and Scotland, and tells facetious stories of gentlemen in both countries; among others, that, in passing near the residence of Sir J. Campbell, at Aghanbrach, he learned that this gentleman had spent a great deal, and was living upon so much per week for an allowance. Hempson through delicacy would not call, but some of the domestics were sent after him. On coming into the castle, Sir J. Campbell asked him why he had not called, adding, 'Sir, there never was a harper but yourself that passed the door of my father's house.' To which Hempson answered, 'that he had heard in the neighbourhood his honor was not often at home;' with which delicate evasion Sir J. was satisfied. He adds, 'that this was the stateliest and highest bred man he ever knew; if he were putting on a new pair of gloves, and one of them dropped on the floor, (though ever so clean,) he would order the servant to bring another pair.' He says that in that time he never met but one laird who had a harp, and that was a very small one, played formerly by the laird's father;[a] and that when he had tuned it with new strings, the laird and his lady were so pleased with his music, that they invited him back in these words: 'Hempson, as soon as you think this child of ours (a boy of three years of age) is fit to learn on his grandfather's harp, come back to teach him, and you shall not repent it;' but this he never accomplished. He told me a story of the Laird of Strone, with a great deal of comic relish. When he was playing at the house, a messenger came, that a large party of gentlemen were coming to grouse, and would spend some days with him, (the laird.) The lady, being in great distress, turned to her husband, saying, 'What shall we do, my dear, for so many, in the way of beds?' 'Give yourself no uneasiness,' replied the laird; 'give us enough to eat,

[a] Very probably the Lude Harp.

and I will supply the rest; and as for beds, believe me, *every man shall find one for himself,'* (meaning, that his guests would fall under the table.)

"In his second trip to Scotland, in the year 1745, he was at that time, by his own account, nearly fifty years of age: being at Edinburgh when Charley the Pretender was there, he was called into the great hall to play; at first he was alone, afterwards four fiddlers joined; the tune called for was, 'The king shall enjoy his own again:' he sung here part of the words following:

"'I hope to see the day
When the Whigs shall run away,
And the king shall enjoy his own again.'

I asked him if he heard the Pretender speak; he replied, I only heard him ask, 'Is Sylvan there?' On which some one answered, 'He is not here, please your Royal Highness, but he shall be sent for.' He meant to say *Sullivan*, continued Hempson, but that was the way he called the name. He says that Captain Macdonald, when in Ireland, came to see him, and that he told the Captain that Charley's cockade was in his father's house.

"Hempson was brought into the Pretender's presence by Colonel Kelly, of Roscommon, and Sir Thomas Sheridan. He played in many Irish houses; among others, those of Lord de Courcy, Mr. Fortescue, Sir P. Bellew, Squire Roche; and in the great towns, Dublin, Cork, &c. &c., respecting all which, he interspersed pleasant anecdotes with surprising gaiety and correctness.

"General Hart, who was an admirer of music, sent a painter to take a drawing of him, which cannot fail to be interesting, if it were only for the venerable expression of his meagre blind countenance, and the symmetry of his tall, thin, but not debilitated person. I found him lying on his back in bed, near the fire of his cabin; his family employed in the usual way; his harp under the bed clothes, by which his face was covered also. When he heard my name, he started up, (being already dressed,) and seemed rejoiced to hear the sound of my voice, which, he said, he began to recollect. He asked for my children, whom I brought to see him, and he felt them over and over; then, with tones of great affection, he blessed God that he had *seen* four generations of the name, and ended by giving the children his blessing. He then tuned his old time-beaten harp, his solace and bed-fellow, and played with astonishing justness and good taste.

"The tunes which he played were his favourites; and he, with an elegance of manner, said at the same time, 'I remember you have a fondness for music, and the tunes you used to ask for I have not forgotten,' which were 'Coolin,' 'The Dawning of the Day,' 'Ellen a Roon,' 'Cean dubh dilis,' &c. These, except the third, were the first tunes which, according to regulation, he played at the famous meeting of harpers at Belfast, under the patronage of some amateurs of Irish music. Mr. Bunting, the celebrated musician of that town, was here in 1793, the year after the meeting, at Hempson's, noting his tunes and his manner of playing, which is in the best old style. He said, with the honest feeling of self-love, 'When I played the old tunes, not another of the harpers would play after me.' He came to Magilligan many years ago, and at the age of eighty-six married a woman of Innishowen, whom he found living in the house of a friend. 'I can't tell,' said Hempson, if it was not the devil buckled us together, she being lame, and I blind.' By this wife he has one daughter, married to a cooper, who has several children, and maintains them all, though Hempson (in this alone seeming to doat) says, that his son-in-law is a spendthrift, and that he maintains them; the family humour his whim, and the old man is quieted. He is pleased when they tell him, as he thinks is the case, that several people of character for musical taste send letters to invite him; and he, though incapable now of leaving the house, is planning expeditions, never to be attempted, much less realized: these are the only traces of mental debility. As to his body, he has no inconvenience but that arising from a chronic disorder. His habits have ever been sober; his favourite drink, once beer, now milk and water; his diet chiefly *potatoes*. I asked him to teach my daughter, but he declined; adding, however, that it was too hard for a young girl, but nothing would give him greater pleasure, if he thought it could be done.

"Lord Bristol, when lodging at the bathing-house of Mount Salut, near Magilligan, gave three guineas, and ground rent free, to build the house where Hempson now lives. At the house-warming, his lordship with his lady and family came, and the children danced to his harp."

It will be satisfactory to such as take an interest in the simple annals of the harpers, and venerate any vestiges of the bardic system, to learn, that the close of Hempson's long life of 112 years (he died in 1807) was rendered comfortable by the humanity of the Rev. Sir H. Harvey Bruce, from whose hand he was often literally fed. The day before his death, upon hearing that this gentleman had come to his cabin, he desired to be raised up in his bed, and the harp placed in his hands. Having struck some notes of a favourite strain, he sunk back unable to proceed, taking his last adieu of an instrument which had been a companion, even in his sleeping hours, and was his hourly solace through a life protracted to the longest span. His harp is preserved in Sir Henry's mansion, at Downhill, as a relic of its interesting owner.[a] It was made by Cormac O'Kelly, about the year 1700, at Ballynascreen, in the county

[a] The following lines are sculptured on it:

"In the days of Noah I was green;
After his flood I've not been seen
Until seventeen hundred and two, I was found,
By Cormac Kelly, under ground;
He raised me up to that degree,
Queen of Music they call me."

The sides and front are made of white sallow, the back of bog fir, patched with copper and iron plates. Quin's harp was made by the same artist. The Editor saw it at Egan's, the late harp maker's, in Dublin. It was a handsomely formed instrument, and made, as usual, of red sallow from the bog. It bears date 1707.

Derry; a district long famous for the construction of such instruments, and for the preservation of ancient Irish melodies in their original purity.[a] It was with great difficulty the Editor was able to procure the old harp music from Hempson. When asked to play the very antique tunes, he uniformly replied, "there was no use in doing so, they were too hard to learn, they revived painful recollections." In short, he regarded the old music with a superstitious veneration, and thought it, in some sort, a profanation to divulge it to modern ears.

Some curious tales are told of JEROME DUIGENAN, a Leitrim harper, born A. D. 1710. One is of so extraordinary a character, that, were it not for the particularity of the details, which savour strongly of an origin in fact, the Editor would hesitate to give it publicity. He is, however, persuaded that he has it as it was communicated to O'Neill, between whose time and that of Duigenan there was scarcely room for the invention of a story not substantially true. It is as follows. "There was a harper," says O'Neill,[b] before my time, named Jerome Duigenan, not blind, an excellent Greek and Latin scholar, and a charming performer. I have heard numerous anecdotes of him. The one that pleased me most was this. He lived with a Colonel Jones, of Drumshambo, who was one of the representatives in parliament for the county of Leitrim. The Colonel, being in Dublin at the meeting of parliament, met with an English nobleman, who had brought over a Welsh harper. When the Welshman had played some tunes before the Colonel, which he did very well, the nobleman asked him had he ever heard so sweet a finger. 'Yes,' replied Jones, 'and that by a man who never wears either linen or woollen.' 'I'll bet you a hundred guineas,' says the nobleman, 'you can't produce any one to excel my Welshman.' The bet was accordingly made, and Duigenan was written to, to come immediately to Dublin, and bring his harp and dress of *Cauthack* with him; that is, a dress made of beaten rushes, with something like a caddy or plaid of the same stuff. On Duigenan's arrival in Dublin, the Colonel acquainted the members with the nature of his bet, and they requested that it might be decided *in the House of Commons*, before business commenced. The two harpers performed before all the members accordingly, and it was unanimously decided in favour of Duigenan, who wore his full *Cauthack* dress, and a cap of the same stuff, shaped like a sugar loaf, with many tassels; he was a tall, handsome man, and looked very well in it." Unquestionably this sugar-loaf cap was the *barrad* of the old bards,[c] and corresponds with the costume of the head carved on the extremity of the forearm of Mr. Dalway's harp, represented in the Editor's former volume, as well as on that made by Kelly, of Ballynascreen, in 1726, and figured in Walker's Memoirs.

CHARLES BYRNE, another Leitrim man, born about 1712, was one of those who attended the Belfast Meeting. Although not distinguished as a performer, he possessed an extraordinary fund of songs and anecdotes, of which the Editor has availed himself to a considerable extent.

[a] The beautiful tunes, "Sliebh Gallen" and "The Little Swallow," are two of them: they are now given to the world for the first time.

[b] O'Neill MS.

[c] Walker, p. 15.

O'SHEA, a County Kerry harper, was born in the same year. He possessed considerable abilities, and was an enthusiast in every thing connected with Irish feeling : extreme debility alone prevented him attending the Belfast Meeting.

The next in the list is DOMINIC MUNGAN, long famous for his excellent performance throughout the North of Ireland, where he regularly went the North-West circuit with the bar. He was born about 1715, a native of that pastoral and poetical county, Tyrone, and blind from his birth. He had three sons, the youngest of whom, Mark, after giving promise of great excellence as a scholar, died early in life ; another, John, a physician, rose to eminence in his profession in the county of Monaghan ; and the third, Terence, attained to the distinguished position, first, of Dean of Ardagh, and finally of Bishop of Limerick, in the Established Church. Dominic was himself a man of prudence and economy, which enabled him to put his sons in the way of preferment, by securing them a good education. He was a most admirable performer. Those janglings of the strings so general among ordinary practitioners were never heard from the harp in his hands. But it was in the piano passages he chiefly excelled; these came out with an effect indescribably charming. His "whispering notes" were, until lately, in the memory of a few surviving auditors ; they commenced in a degree of piano that required the closest approach to the instrument to render them at first audible, but increased by degrees to the richest chords. In their greatest degree of softness, they resembled rather the sympathetic tones than those brought out by the finger. Dominic was conversant with the best music of his day, that of Corelli, Handel, and Geminiani, select *adagios* from which he often played. Of the vocal airs of Handel, he preferred the song of "Let me wander not unseen," and played it delightfully. He had also paid considerable attention to sacred music, and, as might be expected from the purity of his taste, preferred the hundredth psalm to all others. The late Henry Joy, Esq., of Belfast, to whose valuable assistance the Editor is much indebted in this and the former volume of this work, had often heard him play, and it is on his authority that the above observations have been put forward.

DANIEL BLACK, a harper from Derry who attended the Belfast Meeting, was born about the same time with Mungan. His chief resort, when in Antrim, was Mr. Heyland's seat at Glendaragh, near Antrim, where the Editor saw him shortly before his death, in 1796. He sung to the harp very sweetly.

A much more celebrated character was ECHLIN (or ACKLAND) KANE, born at Drogheda, 1720. He was a scholar of Lyons, and did credit to that great harper's teaching. His love of adventure early led him to Rome, where he played before the Pretender, then resident there ; he afterwards travelled into France and Spain, where the Irish, of whom there were at that time a great number residing in Madrid, patronized him very liberally, and introduced him to the notice of his Catholic Majesty, who is said to have contemplated settling a pension on him, in compliment to his countrymen. Kane's preferment was, however, marred by his own indiscretions ; and, after exhausting the patronage of his countrymen at the Spanish Court, he was obliged to set out for Bilboa, on his way home, on foot, and carrying his harp on his back. He is described as a very strong, tall, and athletic man, and is asserted to have outstripped the post on this journey, which may appear the less extraordinary when the state of the roads in Spain at the time is considered. He does not appear to have spent much time in Ireland, for we find him very famous throughout Scotland for a long period before his death, which occurred some time about 1790. His chief haunts in Scotland were about Blair-Athol, and Dunkeld; but he was also widely known throughout the Lowlands and Isles. In a tour through the Isles in 1775, he was at Lord Macdonald's, of Skye, where he recommended himself so much by his performance, that Lord Macdonald presented him with a silver harp-key that had long been in the family, being unquestionably the key left by his great predecessor and namesake, Rory Dall. Echlin, however, does not appear to have been always equally successful in recommending himself to the good offices of his patrons, for Mr. Gunn relates of him, that the Highland gentry occasionally found it necessary to repress his turbulence by cutting his nails, and so rendering him unable to play, till they grew again to their proper length. Mr. Gunn states that "he was often spoken of by Manini at Cambridge with rapture, as being able (though blind) to play with accuracy and great effect the fine treble and bass parts of many of Corelli's correntos in concert with other music." Had he been but moderately correct in his conduct, Echlin Kane might, unquestionably, have raised the character of the wandering minstrel higher than it had stood for a century before.

Of a lower grade, as a harper, and of even more debased habits, was THADY ELLIOTT, born in the year 1725. The character of the man may be judged of from the fact, that he once, for a trifling wager, struck up "Planxty Connor" in the most solemn part of high mass at the chapel of Navan, where he usually accompanied the service on his harp. Notwithstanding his vices and follies, he was, however, a capital performer, and generous and hospitable in the highest degree.

OWEN KEENAN, also born in the same year, was another of the reckless and turbulent class, which, it is to be regretted, was now more numerous than any other. Still there is a good deal of adventurous interest, if not of genuine romance, in the various escapades and frolics in which he was engaged. Being often at Killymoon, the residence of Mr. Stewart, near Cookstown, in the county of Tyrone, he became enamoured of a French governess who resided with that family; and, blind though he was, contrived on one occasion, like another Romeo, to make his way to her apartment by a ladder. Mr. Stewart, justly offended, had him committed to Omagh gaol on a charge, as is presumed, of housebreaking. There was at that time a very good harper, also blind, called HIGGINS, who was of a respectable family in Tyrawley, County Mayo, and who travelled in a better style than most others of the fraternity; he, hearing of Keenan's mishap, posted down to Omagh, where his appearance and retinue readily procured him admission to the gaol. The gaoler was from home; his wife loved music and cordials; these harpers, too, knew how to humour the amiable weaknesses of one who had been once a beauty. The result may be imagined. The blind men stole the keys out of her pocket, while oppressed with love and music, made the turnkeys drunk, and, while Higgins stayed behind like another Orpheus, charming Cerberus with his lyre, Keenan "marched out by moonlight merrily," with Higgins's boy on his back, to guide him over a ford of the Strule, by which he took his route direct to Killymoon again, scaled the walls once more, and finally, after another commitment for "the ladder business," as O'Neill calls it, and a narrow escape at the county assizes, carried off his Juliet, and married her. Even in America the bardic character, such at least as characterized the harpers of this period, was sustained by Irish wanderers. Keenan, after his marriage, emigrated to the States, where his Juliet, however, proved unfaithful to him; and in Canada, Michael Keane, another of the same musical race with Rory Dall, who had gone out with Mr. Dobbs, of Castle Dobbs, in the county of Antrim, on his appointment as Governor of South Carolina, previous to the declaration of American independence, played pranks as extravagant as any of his cotemporaries. Sir Malby Crofton used to tell this story of him, "That when he and some other officers were garrisoned in Fort Oswego, and had a party, Keane was with them, and quarrelled with them, and beat them very well, and took a Miss Williams from them all."[a]

Hugh O'Neill, the preceptor and friend of Arthur, was, however, like his pupil, an exception to the general character of the harpers of this period. He was born at Foxford, in Mayo, of highly respectable parents; his mother being a Macdonnell, and cousin of the famous Count Taaffe. Having lost his sight by the small-pox, when seven years old, he devoted himself to music at first, as an amusement, and afterwards, in consequence of unexpected losses, as an occupation. The respectability of his family, and propriety of his conduct, gained him the general esteem of the Connaught gentry, among whom he was admitted more as a companion than as a hired performer. To the liberality of Mr. Tennison, of Castle Tennison, in the county of Roscommon, he was indebted for a large farm, at a nominal rent, which he was able to stock and cultivate to advantage. Blind though he was, he used regularly to go out with the hounds, which, in an open grazing country like Roscommon, he could do with comparatively little risk. He was carried off by fever while still a young man, and is buried in Kilronan, in the same grave with Carolan.

Of Arthur O'Neill himself so much has already been said, both in the preface and in the preceding portion of this chapter, that little remains to be added. He was born at Drumnaslad, near Dungannon, in the county of Tyrone, a district still full of poetry and genius, in the year 1734. Having lost his sight by an accident, when two years old, he was early put under the instruction of Owen Keenan, the blind Romeo of Killymoon above-mentioned, with a view to music as a means of livelihood. At the age of fifteen he commenced his own career as an itinerant harper, making his first journey to Mr. Boyd's, of Ballycastle, in the county of Antrim. By the time he was nineteen years old, he had gone the circuit of the four provinces, and had been brought in contact with almost all the chief families both of English and Irish descent in the country. He continued to lead the same sort of life until the year 1807, when,

[a] The O'Neill MS.

on the establishment of the Belfast Irish Harp Society, he was unanimously elected the resident Master of that institution. His memoirs, dictated by himself, abound in curious and interesting particulars, and have been largely used in the compilation of this work. Although his peregrinations extended over all Ireland, his principal haunts were in the southern counties of Ulster, particularly in Cavan, where, during the ten years preceding his election as Master of the Belfast School, his permanent head quarters were at Colonel Southwell's, of Castle-Hamilton. With Philip Reilly, of Mullough, in the same county, he made it a point to spend his Christmas holidays; and at the time of his removal to Belfast, had thus celebrated eighteen successive festivals in the house of his friend. He was also a great favourite of the famous Charles O'Connor, of Belanagar, in the county of Roscommon, and spent much time in his house. From the conversation of this celebrated man, he had acquired a good knowledge of Irish history, on which he prided himself fully as much as on his abilities as a harper. He was a remarkably pleasant companion, abounding in anecdote, and could play both backgammon and cards with great dexterity. He was proud of his descent, and had the *hand* of the O'Neills engraved on his coat buttons, which were of silver, and of half-crown size. When the Harp Society fell to the ground, O'Neill retired to his native county, where he continued to receive an annual stipend from some lovers of native music in Belfast, until his death, which took place near Dungannon, in 1818, in the eighty-fifth year of his age.

Charles Fanning, the cotemporary and rival of O'Neill, was the son of Loughlin Fanning, also a harper, and was born at Foxford, in Mayo, about 1736. His chief haunts were in Ulster, particularly in Cavan, where Mr. Pratt, of Kingscourt, allowed him a free house and farm. He was also patronized by the celebrated Earl of Bristol, the great Bishop of Derry; but in consequence of having married a person in low life, and of corresponding habits, he never attained to respectability or independence.

Harry Fitzsimon, a native of the county of Down, was another of the less respectable class. He and his son Harry, junior, were both excellent performers, but such irreclaimable libertines, that they could not be received into respectable families.

A very different character was Mr. James Duncan, also a native of Down, who had recourse to the harp as a means of defraying the expenses of litigation in which he was engaged, for the recovery of his paternal property. It will gratify the reader to know that by this means he ultimately gained his suit, which was still pending at the time of the Meeting at Belfast, in 1792, when he was one of the candidates, and died about 1800, in the enjoyment of a handsome competence.

Although formerly it was very usual for females to apply themselves to the harp, yet at this epoch there were but two female performers of any repute in Ulster. These were Catherine Martin, a Meath woman, who delighted greatly in the tunes composed by Parson Stirling, of Lurgan;[a] and Rose Mooney, a pupil of Elliot's, who attended the

[a] This gentleman composed many capital airs, which he performed on the bagpipes, but did not cultivate the harp.

Granard and Belfast Meetings. The latter died at Killala, just after the landing of the French there, under very lamentable circumstances.

Of those who attended at Belfast, the youngest, and consequently the last in this list, were Patrick Quin, of Portadown, in the county of Armagh, and William Carr, of the same county; the former born about 1745, the latter in 1777. Quin had been taught by Patrick Linden, of the Fews, County Armagh, a distinguished performer and poet. He was selected to play at the meeting in commemoration of Carolan, held in the Rotunda at Dublin, in 1809, and was so elated by the commendations he received for his performance on that occasion, that, on his return to his own residence, he declined playing any longer on the violin, from which he had hitherto reaped a good harvest, by performing at wakes and merry meetings in his neighbourhood. It is worthy of remark, that Quin was the only harper at the Belfast Meeting who attempted to play "Patrick's Day," of which he was very proud, having set, or, as he expressed it, "fixed it" for the harp.

The foregoing list might readily be swelled to a much greater extent, but it has been deemed better to notice those only of whom something characteristic could be said, or who have made themselves conspicuous by their abilities as composers or performers.

CHAPTER VI.

NOTICES OF THE MORE REMARKABLE PIECES AND MELODIES OF THE COLLECTION.

In the following notices, the arrangement pointed at in the Preface has been followed, the order of the notices, except that of the *prelude* (No. I.), corresponding, as nearly as the Editor's knowledge admits, with the chronological series of the airs referred to. This arrangement, however, has only been adopted to a certain extent in the collection itself, as it is apprehended that, if the melodies of the several classes were given consecutively, a monotonous effect might be produced. This statement will explain any apparent discrepancy in the numbers referred to, under the following notices.

AIRS OF THE FIRST CLASS—VERY ANCIENT.

I. *Feaghan Gleash.* "Try if it be in tune."—An ancient Irish prelude. This extremely curious piece was taken down from Hempson's performance in the year 1792, and is given as he played it. It was with great reluctance that the old harper was prevailed on to play even the fragment of it here preserved, to gratify the Editor, to whom he acknowledged he was under obligations. He would rather, he asserted, have played any other air, as this awakened recollections of the days of his youth, of friends whom he had outlived, and of times long past, when the harpers were accustomed to play the ancient caoinans or lamentations, with their corresponding preludes.[a] When pressed to play, notwithstanding, his peevish answer uniformly was, " What's the use of doing so ? no one can understand it now, not even any of the harpers now living." This relic is but one half of the prelude, as he solemnly averred that he had forgotten the remainder. It is now for ever lost; but what has been preserved will serve, with other curious matters, to shew the great attention formerly paid to every thing connected with music in Ireland. The musical critic is requested to observe two striking peculiarities in this first part of the ancient Irish prelude ; first, the total absence of the chord of the subdominant; and secondly, the evidently premeditated omission of the two intervals of the diatonic scale, the fourth and seventh. Whether the second part of the prelude included these tones or not cannot now be ascertained.

II. *Neaill ghubh a Dheirdre.* " The Lamentation of Deirdre for the Sons of Usnach." —This is, perhaps, the oldest piece in the collection ; for the story of the Death of the Sons of Usnach, in which the lament occurs, ranks in antiquity with that of the Children of Lir, and refers to a period considerably anterior to the Ossianic era. It is hard to say in what particular part of the story the interest lies, which has taken so strong a hold on the imaginations of the people. It would appear, however, to consist mainly in its frequent examples of magnanimity and fortitude, and in the high idea which it gives us of ancient honour. The story, of which it is proposed to give a brief abstract, opens with the birth of the heroine, who was daughter of Felimy, the son of Dall, rhymer to Conor Mac Nessa, King of Ulster. The Druid Cathbad, who was present at her birth, gave her the name of Deirdre, and at the same time prophesied her future misfortunes in stanzas, which have been thus rendered :

" Child of sorrow, sin, and shame,
Deirdre be thy dreaded name !
Child of doom, thy fatal charms
Soon shall work us deadly harms.

Long shall Ulster mourn the night
Gave thine eyes their blasting light;
Long shall Usnach rue the day
Shew'd his sons their fatal ray !"

Accordingly, notwithstanding the precautions of King Conor, who, desiring to educate her for his future queen, had her brought up in the strictest seclusion, she conceives a passion for Naisi, the son of Usnach. Their first interview is thus described in a paraphrase of the original Irish, given in the Hibernian Nights' Entertainments, (*Dublin University Magazine*, December, 1834.) " Now, on a certain day, Naisi was sitting in the midst of the plain of

[a] From an error in the engraving of the music, the arpeggios in this prelude are made to run from the lower to the higher notes, as in the modern style, when they should have been in the contrary direction, according to the practice of the ancient Irish harpers.

Eman, (Emania, near Armagh,) playing on a harp. Sweet, in truth, was the music of the sons of Usnach. The cattle, listening to it, milked ever two-thirds more than was their wont; and all pain and sorrow failed not to depart from whatsoever man or woman heard the strains of that melody. Great, also, was their prowess; when each set his back to the other, all Conor's province had been unable to overcome them. They were fleet as hounds in the chase; they slew deer with their speed. Now, then, as Naisi sat singing on the plain of Eman, he perceived a maiden approaching him. She held down her head as she came near him, and would have passed in silence. 'Gentle is the damsel who passeth by,' said Naisi. Then the maiden, looking up, replied, 'Damsels may well be gentle where there are no youths.' Then Naisi knew it was Deirdre, and great dread fell upon it. 'The king of the province is betrothed to thee, oh damsel,' he said. 'I love him not,' she replied; 'he is an aged man, I would rather love a youth like thee.' 'Say not so, oh damsel,' said Naisi; 'the king is a better spouse than the king's servant.' 'Thou sayest so,' said Deirdre, 'that thou mayest avoid me.' Then plucking a rose from a briar, she flung it towards him, and said, 'Now art thou ever disgraced, if thou rejectest me.' 'Depart from me, I beseech thee, damsel,' said Naisi. 'If thou dost not take me to be thy wife,' said Deirdre, 'thou art dishonoured before all the men of thy country, after what I have done.' Then Naisi said no more; and Deirdre took the harp, and sat beside him playing sweetly. But the sons of Usnach, rushing forth, came running to the spot where Naisi sat, and Deirdre with him. 'Alas!" they cried, 'what hast thou done, oh brother? Is not this damsel fated to ruin Ulster?' 'I am disgraced before the men of Erin for ever,' said Naisi, 'if I take her not after that which she hath done.' 'Evil will come of it,' said the brothers. 'I care not,' said Naisi,' 'I had rather be in misfortune than in dishonour; we will fly with her to another country.' * * * So that night they departed, taking with them three times fifty men of might, and three times fifty women, and three times fifty greyhounds, and three times fifty attendants; and Naisi took Deirdre to be his wife."

After wandering through various parts of Ireland, "from Easroe to Ben Edar, and from Dundelgan to Almhuin," the fugitives at length took shelter in Scotland, where they found an asylum on the banks of Loch Etive. The loss of three warriors of such repute soon began to be felt by the nobles of Ulster, who found themselves no longer able to make head with their accustomed success against the southern provinces. They, therefore, urged Conor to abandon his resentment, and recal the fugitives. Conor, with no other intention than that of re-possessing himself of Deirdre, feigned compliance. But to induce Clan Usnach (so the fugitives were called) to trust themselves again in the hands of him whom their leader had so outraged, it was necessary that the message of pardon should be borne by one on whose warranty of safe conduct the most implicit reliance could be reposed. After sounding some of his chief nobles who were of sufficient authority to undertake the mission, among the rest Cuchullin, and finding that any attempt to tamper with them would be unavailing, Conor fixes on Fergus, the son of Roy, as a more likely instrument, and commits the embassy to him. But though he does not so much fear the consequences of compromising the safe conduct of Fergus, as of Cuchullin, or the others, he yet does not venture openly to enlist him in the meditated treachery, but proceeds by a stratagem, which in these days may appear somewhat far-fetched, yet probably was not inconsistent with the manners of that time. Fergus was of the order of the Red Branch, and the brethren of the Red Branch were under vow not to refuse hospitality at one another's hands. Conor, therefore, arranged with Barach, one of his minions, and a brother of the order, to intercept Fergus on his return, by the tender of a three days' banquet, well knowing that the Clan Usnach must in that case proceed to Emania without the presence of their protector. Meanwhile, Fergus arriving in the harbour of Loch Etive, where dwelt Clan Usnach in green hunting booths along the shore, "sends forth the loud cry of a mighty man of chase." Then follows a characteristic passage. Deirdre and Naisi sat together in their tent, and Conor's polished chess-board between them. And Naisi hearing the cry, said, "I hear the call of a man of Erin." "That was not the call of a man of Erin," replied Deirdre, "but the call of a man of Alba." Then again Fergus shouted a second time. "Surely that was the call of a man of Erin," said Naisi. "Surely no," said Deirdre, "let us play on." Then again Fergus shouted a third time, and Naisi knew that it was the cry of Fergus, and he said, "If the son of Roy be in existence, I hear his hunting shout from the Loch; go forth Ardan, my brother, and give our kinsman welcome." "Alas," cried Deirdre, "I knew the call of Fergus from the first!" For she has a prophetic dread that foul play is intended them, and this feeling never subsides in her breast from that hour till the catastrophe. Quite different are the feelings of Naisi; he reposes the most unlimited confidence in the safe conduct vouched for by his brother in arms, and, in spite of the remonstrances of Deirdre, embarks with all his retainers for Ireland. Deirdre, on leaving the only secure or happy home she ever expects to enjoy, sings a pathetic farewell, the words of which vary considerably in different copies. It is thus versified in the paper above alluded to:

"Farewell to fair Alba, high house of the sun;
Farewell to the mountain, the cliff, and the dun;
Dun Sweeny, adieu! for my love cannot stay,
And tarry I must not, when love cries away.

Glen Vashan! Glen Vashan! where roebucks run free,
Where my love used to feast on the red deer with me,
Where, rocked on thy waters, while stormy winds blew,
My love used to slumber; Glen Vashan, adieu!

Glendaro! Glendaro! where birchen boughs weep
Honey dew at high noon to the nightingale's sleep;
Where my love used to lead me to hear the cuckoo,
'Mong the high hazel bushes; Glendaro, adieu!

Glenurchy! Glenurchy! where loudly and long
My love used to wake up the woods with his song,
While the son of the rock,[a] from the depths of the dell,
Laughed sweetly in answer; Glenurchy, farewell!

Glen Etive! Glen Etive! where dappled does roam,
Where I leave the green sheeling, I first call'd a home,
Where with me my true love delighted to dwell,
The sun made his mansion;[b] Glen Etive, farewell!

Farewell to Inch Draynagh; adieu to the roar
Of blue billows bursting in light on the shore;
Dun Fiagh, farewell! for my love cannot stay,
And tarry I must not when love cries 'away.'"

[a] "Son of the rock." The echo.

[b] She calls Glen Etive *Bally-Graine*, or "Suntown."

Barach meets them on their landing, and detains Fergus, who reluctantly assigns his charge to his two sons, Red Buini Borb and Illan Finn, to conduct them in safety to their journey's end. Deirdre's fears are more and more excited; she has dreams and visions of disasters : she urges Naisi to go to Dunseverick or to Dundalgan, (Dundalk, the residence of Cuchullin,) and there await the coming up of Fergus. Naisi is inflexible. It would injure the honour of his companion in arms to admit any apprehension of danger while under his pledge of safe conduct. The omens multiply ; Deirdre's sense of danger becomes more and more acute. Still Naisi's reply is, "I fear not, let us proceed." At length they reach Emania, and are assigned the House of the Red Branch for their lodging. Calm, and to all appearance unconscious of any cause for apprehension, Naisi takes his place at the chess-table, and Deirdre, full of fears, sits opposite. Meanwhile the king, knowing that Deirdre was again within his reach, could not rest at the banquet, but sends spies to bring him word "if her beauty yet lived upon her." The first messenger, friendly to Clan Usnach, reports that she is "quite bereft of her own aspect, and is lovely and desirable no longer." This allays Conor's passion for a time, but growing heated with wine, he shortly after sends another messenger, who brings back the intelligence, that not only is Deirdre "the fairest woman on the ridge of the world," but that he himself has been wounded by Naisi, who had resented his gazing in at the window of the Red Branch, by flinging a chess-man at his head, and dashing out one of his eyes.[a] This was all that Conor wanted ; he starts up in pretended indignation at the violence done his servant, calls his body-guard, and attacks the Red Branch. The defence now devolves on the sons of Fergus. Clan Usnach scorn to evince alarm, or interfere in any way with the duties of their protectors. But Deirdre cannot conceal her consciousness that they are betrayed, "Ah me," she cries, hearing the soldiery of Conor at the gates, "I knew that Fergus was a traitor." "If Fergus hath betrayed you," replied Red Buini Borb, "yet will not I betray you." And he issues out, and slays his "thrice fifty men of might." But when Conor offers him Slieve Fuadh for a bribe, he holds back his hand from the slaughter, and goes his way. Then cries Deirdre, "Traitor father, traitor son." "No," replies Illan Finn, "though Red Buini Borb be a traitor, yet will not I be a traitor ; while liveth this small straight sword in my hand, I will not forsake Clan Usnach !" Then Illan Finn, encountering Fiara, the son of Conor, armed with Ocean, Flight, and Victory, the royal shield, spear, and sword ; they fight "a fair fight, stout and manly, bitter and bloody, savage and hot, and vehement and terrible, until the waves round the blue rim of Ocean roared, for it was the nature of Conor's shield that it ever resounded as with the noise of stormy waters when he who bore it was in danger." Summoned by which signal, one of King Conor's nobles, coming behind Illan Finn, thrusts him through. "The weakness of death then fell darkly upon Illan, and he threw his arms into the mansion, and called to Naisi to fight manfully, and expired." Clan Usnach at length deign to lay aside their chess-tables,

[a] Chess-men were formerly made of a much larger size than in our time. The Archæologia contains a curious account of a massive set of chess-men, made of the tooth of the sea horse.

and stand to their arms. Ardan first sallies out, and slays his "three hundred men of might;" then Ainli, who makes twice that havoc; and last, Naisi himself: and, "till the sands of the sea, the dewdrops of the meadows, the leaves of the forest, or the stars of heaven be counted, it is not possible to tell the number of heads and hands, and lopped limbs of heroes that then lay bare and red from the hands of Naisi and his brothers on that plain." Then Naisi came again into the Red Branch to Deirdre; and she encouraged him, und said, "We will yet escape: fight manfully, and fear not." Then the sons of Usnach made a phalanx of their shields, and spread the links of their joined bucklers round Deirdre, and bounding forth like three eagles, swept down upon the troops of Conor, making sore havoc of his people. Now when Cathbad, the druid, saw that the sons of Usnach were bent on the destruction of Conor himself, he had recourse to his arts of magic; and he cast an enchantment over them, so that their arms fell from their hands, and they were taken by the men of Ulster, for the spell was like a sea of thick gums about them, and their limbs were clogged in it, that they could not move. The sons of Usnach are then put to death, and Deirdre, standing over the grave, sings their funeral song, which is thus rendered:

"The lions of the hill are gone,
And I am left alone—alone;
Dig the grave both wide and deep,
For I am sick, and fain would sleep.

The falcons of the wood are flown,
And I am left alone—alone;
Dig the grave both deep and wide,
And let us slumber side by side.

The dragons of the rock are sleeping,
Sleep that wakes not for our weeping;
Dig the grave, and make it ready,
Lay me on my true love's body.

Lay their spears and bucklers bright
By the warriors' sides aright;
Many a day the three before me
On their linkéd bucklers bore me.

Lay upon the low grave floor,
'Neath each head, the blue claymore;
Many a time the noble three
Reddened these blue blades for me.

Lay the collars, as is meet,
Of their greyhounds at their feet;
Many a time for me have they
Brought the tall red deer to bay.

In the falcon's jesses throw,
Hook and arrow, line and bow;
Never again by stream or plain
Shall the gentle woodsmen go.

Sweet companions, were ye ever
Harsh to me your sister, never;
Woods and wilds, and misty valleys
Were with you as good 's a palace.

Oh! to hear my true love singing,
Sweet as sounds of trumpets' ringing;
Like the sway of ocean swelling
Rolled his deep voice round our dwelling.

Oh! to hear the echoes pealing
Round our green and fairy sheeling,
When the three with soaring chorus
Made the skylark silent o'er us!

Echo now sleep morn and even;
Lark, alone enchant the heaven;
Ardan's lips are scant of breath,
Naisi's tongue is cold in death.

Stag, exult on glen and mountain;
Salmon, leap from loch to fountain;
Heron, in the free air warm ye,
Usnach's sons no more will harm ye.

Erin's stay, no more ye are
Rulers of the ridge of war;
Never more 'twill be your fate
To keep the beam of battle straight.

Woe is me! by fraud and wrong,
Traitors false, and tyrants strong,
Fell Clan Usnach, bought and sold
For Barach's feast and Conor's gold.

Woe to Eman, roof and wall!
Woe to Red Branch, hearth and hall!
Tenfold woe and black dishonour
To the foul and false Clan Conor.

Dig the grave both wide and deep,
Sick I am, and fain would sleep!
Dig the grave, and make it ready,
Lay me on my true love's body."

So saying, she flung herself into the grave, and expired. Such is an outline of this tale, which has possessed an extraordinary charm for the people of Ireland for now better than a thousand years.

III. "The Caoinans."—The Irish Cry, as sung in Ulster, together with the Great and Little Cry, appear to claim a place in this class, as well from the antique air which pervades their structure, as from the fact of the Goll chanted by a single voice, being still sung to words referred to the tenth century.—(See Preface, p. 7.) The present set was procured from professed Keeners in the county of Armagh.—(See another set of "The Caoinan," No. 59, in the Collection.)

IV. "Ballinderry."—From what has already been stated respecting this air, it is hoped that the musical reader will be prepared to regard it with considerable interest. The *cronan* or chorus, which imparts its great peculiarity to the piece, will be found to form a tolerably perfect bass, except in the last bar, which wants the cadence to make it complete. It has been a favourite performance from time immemorial with the peasantry of the counties of Down and Antrim, the words being sung by one person, while the rest of the party chant the *cronan* in consonance. There are several other Irish airs with a similar chorus, but the Editor has not succeeded in finding any other in which the *cronan* forms a bass, or harmonizes with the air, as it does in this. The words, which are at present most popular with the air, will be found accompanying it. There are numerous other sets of words sung to "Ballinderry;" they are all of a very rustic character, and uniformly refer to localities along the rivers Bann and Lagan, such as,

"'Tis pretty to be in Ballinderry,
'Tis pretty to be at Magheralin," &c.

"'Tis pretty to be in Ballinderry,
'Tis pretty to be at the Cash of Toome," &c.

V. "Argan Mór."—An Ossianic air, still sung to the words preserved by Dr. Young, and published in the first volume of the Transactions of the Royal Irish Academy. The Editor took down the notes from the singing, or rather recitation, of a native of Murloch, in the county of Antrim. This sequestered district lies along the sea shore, between Tor Point and Fairhead, and is still rife with tradition, both musical and legendary. From the neighbouring ports of Cushendun and Cushendall was the principal line of communication with Scotland, and doubtless it was by this very route that the Ossianic poems themselves originally travelled into the country of Macpherson.

The Air repeated to each Stanza of the Poem.

B introduced by the Editor.

THE BATTLE OF ARGAN MORE

These Airs are repeated to each stanza of the Poems.

SCOTT'S LAMENTATION

AS ORIGINALLY PERFORMED BY HEMPSON ON THE IRISH HARP.

Mæl: ♪ = 120 — Pen: 8 Inches. Composed in 1599.

VI. " Ossianic Air."—Communicated by Sir John Sinclair, Bart., from whose letter to the Editor, the following is an extract:

" Charlotte-square, Edinburgh, 30*th August*, 1808.

" A remnant of the music to which the poems of Ossian were anciently sung was recently transmitted to me by the Rev. Mr. Cameron, Minister of Halkirk, in the county of Caithness, North Britain, who learned it many years ago from a very old man, a farmer on my estate, who was accustomed to sing some of Ossian's poems to that air, with infinite delight and enthusiasm. Every connoisseur in music must perceive at once that, from its simplicity, wildness, and peculiar structure, it must be a very ancient composition, and it is probably the oldest piece of music extant.

" With my best wishes for your success in your laudable exertions to collect and to give to the public the ancient melodies of the Celtic tribes who inhabited Ireland and the northern parts of Scotland, tribes who resembled each other so much in language, in manners, in the music which they sung, and the valour with which they fought, that they may be considered as one people.

" I remain, dear Sir,
" Your humble and very obedient Servant,
" John Sinclair."

VII. " Scott's Lamentation."—With the original bass and treble, as played by Hempson, precisely as he learned it from Bridget O'Cahan. This specimen probably belongs to that highly finished school of performance which so much excited the admiration of Giraldus in the twelfth century.

AIRS OF THE SECOND CLASS—ANCIENT.

In noticing the more remarkable airs of the second or less ancient class, it seems proper to begin with such as are of ascertained origin; and it will be observed, that between the date of the first of these, excepting the Coolun, and the era to which the preceding class has been assigned, there is a very long interval. To this interval very probably belong some of the melodies of unascertained date included in the same class, but postponed in the order of their notices to those of more certain origin.

I. (No. 119 in the Collection.) " Coolun."—This far-famed melody is here given as it was played by Hempson, who had learned his set of it, with variations, from Lyons. The style will be found even more Irish than that of the sets hitherto published, though these have been so instrumental in making the world acquainted with the peculiar air and sentiment of our national melodies. The " Coolun" is popularly understood to be a composition of the time of Henry the Eighth, in the twenty-eighth year of whose reign, says Mr. Moore, an Act was passed prohibiting the wearing of those long locks of hair on the back of the head so designated, "on which occasion a song was written by one of our bards, in which an

Irish virgin is made to give the preference to her dear Coulin (or youth with the flowing locks) to all strangers." From a learned paper, by Mr. Lynch, in the first volume of the *Dublin Penny Journal*, (p. 335,) it would, however, appear that the Act referred to was passed so early as A. D. 1295, to which remote period the composition of the air and words is consequently referrible. The Act in question recites, that "the English, being in a manner degenerate, have of late clothed themselves in Irish raiment, and having their heads half shaved, nourish and prolong the hair from the back of the head, calling it *Culan*, conforming to the Irish as well in face and aspect as in dress, whereby it oftentimes happens that certain English, being mistaken for Irishmen, are slain, albeit that the slaying of an Englishman and the slaying of an Irishman are crimes which demand different modes of punishment, by reason whereof great cause of enmity and rancour is generated amongst many persons, and the kinsmen of the slayer as well as of the slain do frequently fall at feud. Be it therefore," &c., &c. A good specimen of the *Coolun* is seen in the figure of the harper from the cross at Ullard, in Chap. III.

II. (No. 123 in the Collection.) *Eibhlin a Ruin.* "Ellen a Roon."—This air, of which so much has been said, is undoubtedly pure Irish, but not in the form in which it has been given by various publishers. It was sung by an Italian named Leoni, in Dublin, about sixty years ago, with Irish words commencing, "Ducca tu non vanatu Eibhlin a Ruin," in which setting the music was altered, to suit the taste of the Italian singer ; but in the setting now given, taken from Hempson's performance, it is restored to its original simplicity, as arranged by *Lyons* the harper. This air embraces all the intervals of the diatonic scale ; the only peculiarity in its composition is the frequent recurrence of the fourth tone, which makes it rank, in the Editor's opinion, in antiquity equal to "The Coolun" and "The Summer is coming," and places it long prior to the latter end of the sixteenth and beginning of the seventeenth century, when the fourth tone of the scale seems to have been designedly omitted in the compositions of the Scotts, O'Cahan, and other composers of that period.

III. (No. 68 in the Collection.) *Maire óg ná gciabh.* "Young Mary of the Tresses."—The words bear internal marks of a very high antiquity ; thus in the third stanza :

> "By the melodious charm of her voice
> She would bring the green sea calf from the wave,
> The dusky wild boar from the misty mountain,
> And the pretty thrush out of the thicket."

The wild boar has not been seen in Ireland for many hundred years.

IV. (No. 8 in the Collection.) "*Cumha Caoine an Albanaigh,*" or Scott's Lamentation for Purcell, Baron of Loughmoe, who died about A. D. 1599. The Purcells were at this time a family of great consideration in the midland counties ; they were allied to the Fitzpatricks, Earls of Upper Ossory, and had six castles in the county of Kilkenny. The Caoine was a solemn piece of music, intended as a tribute of respect to the deceased, and was looked on as the greatest test of the abilities of the harper. It consisted of three divisions in one lesson, and was not intended to be sung. It will be observed, that throughout this piece, the arrangement of which certainly exhibits a vast deal of art and energy, the fourth tone of the diatonic scale never once occurs. So artfully, however, has its omission been managed, that it is not until the notes are closely examined, that its absence is detected. Unquestionably this omission was not the result of any necessity arising from imperfection of the instrument, for at this period the harp is on all hands admitted to have had a compass equal to most stringed instruments of the present day; so that we can only account for the peculiarity by attributing it to the fashion of the time; an explanation supported very strongly by the fact, that in all Rory Dall O'Cahan's pieces composed very shortly after, the tone of the subdominant or fourth is studiously avoided. Most probably the omission was supposed to heighten the effect, by making the Mediant or third tone of the diatonic scale more emphatic. How long before this period the omission of the fourth was prevalent, it is impossible to say, but unquestionably the scale was perfect at the time of the composition of the "Summer is coming," the "Coolun," "If to a foreign clime you go," and many other airs of the thirteenth and fourteenth centuries.

V. (No. 122 in the Collection.) *Cumha an Devenish.* "The Lamentation of Youths." —Another Caoine of Scott's, composed in memory of Hussey, Baron of Galtrim, who died A. D. 1603. It also consists of three parts or divisions, and abounds with those peculiar graces of performance alluded to in Chapter II. The Editor noted it down from the performance of Dominic O'Donnell, a harper from Foxford, in Mayo, who appeared totally unconscious of the art with which he was playing. This air differs from the preceding Caoine by its embracing all the intervals of the diatonic scale.

VI. (No. 13 in the Collection.) *Seabhac na h-Eirnè.* "The Hawk of Ballyshannon," or "O'Moore's Daughter;" an altered composition of Rory Dall, being his "Port Atholl" somewhat varied by Carolan, who composed words to it for Miss Moore. It was uniformly attributed to its proper composer by the harpers at Belfast. *Da Mihi Manum,* (No. 63 in the Collection,) or *Tabhair damh do lamh,* "Give me your hand," is another piece by this famous harper; the occasion which gave rise to its composition has been mentioned in the notice of his life. *Bacach buidhe na leimne,* or the "Yellow Beggar," (No. 20 in the Collection,) is a third by the same eminent hand, and is said to have been composed by him in reference to his own fallen fortunes towards the end of his career.

VII. (No. 2 in the Collection.) *Bantighearna Iveagh.* "Lady Iveagh."—An air remarkable for its haughty and majestic style, suited most probably to the rank and character of the lady to whom it was addressed. The Lady Iveagh, whose name is preserved in this characteristic melody, was Sarah, daughter of Hugh O'Neill, the great Earl of Tyrone. She was married to Art Roe Magennis, who was created Viscount Iveagh by patent of July 18th, 1623.

VIII. (No. 112 in the Collection.) *Máirseail Alasdroinn.* "Macdonnell's March."— This air is mentioned in a note to Smith's History of Cork, vol. ii. p. 159, in the following words: "There is a very odd kind of music well known in Munster by the name of Mac-

Allisdrum's March, being a wild rhapsody made in honor of this commander, to this day much esteemed by the Irish, and played at all their feasts." This was Alister or Alexander Macdonnell, son of Coll Kittogh or "Left handed Coll;" a warrior whose name has been preserved by Milton:

"Why, it is harder, Sirs, than Gordon,
Colkitto, or Macdonnell, or Galasp."

And even more imperishably by vivid traditions of his valour and prowess, handed down to this day, among the Highlanders of Scotland, and the glensmen of the lower part of the county of Antrim. Alister, called also "Young Colkitto," rivalled his father in military fame. He commanded Lord Antrim's Irish, under Montrose, to most of whose victories his courage and conduct mainly contributed. After the breaking up of Montrose's army, Macdonnell and his Irish returned to this country, and joined the standard of the confederate Catholics under Lord Taaffe, in Munster, where a period was put to their exploits by the fatal battle of Knockinoss, 28th September, 1647. After the rout of the main body of the Irish, Macdonnell and his people held their ground till they were cut to pieces by the English. It is said that none escaped. We may form some idea of the desperate courage which inspired these men from the impetuous energy and wild shrilly fervour of this strain, which is undoubtedly the same *pibroch* that they marched to on the morning of their last battle. Macdonnell himself lies buried near Kanturk, in the county of Cork, and his sword, which had a steel apple running in a groove on the back, by means of which its force in striking was greatly increased, is said still to be preserved in Loghan Castle, in the county of Tipperary.

IX. (No. 144 in the Collection.) *Caoine for O'Reilly.*—The O'Reilly, in commemoration of whom this melody was arranged, was Maolmordha, or Miles, sirnamed "The Slasher," probably the son of Maolmordha Dha, or Miles "the handsome," who was "the Queen's O'Reilly" in the reign of Elizabeth. Miles "the Slasher" was colonel of horse in the army commanded by Lord Castlehaven in the wars which followed the rebellion of 1641, and was slain valiantly defending the bridge of Finea against Monro's Scotch, in 1644.—(See Castlehaven's Memoirs.)

X. (No. 98 in the Collection.) *An Londubh.* "The Blackbird."—A very fine air, used as a vehicle for Jacobite words (of which the following verse is a specimen) during the war of 1688-90. The air itself bears evident marks of a much higher antiquity.

"Once in fair England my Blackbird did flourish,
He was the chief flower that in it did spring;
Prime ladies of honour his person did nourish,
Because that he was the true son of a king.
But this false fortune,
Which still is uncertain,
Has caused this long parting between him and me.
His name I'll advance
In Spain and in France,
And seek out my Blackbird wherever he be."

XI. (No. 42 in the Collection.) *Druimindubh.* "The Black-backed Cow."—Another air of high antiquity, adopted as a party tune during these wars; the "black-backed cow" representing, by a very whimsical metaphor, the cause of the exiled monarch. The following stanzas give a good idea of the rude original.

I.

"Ah *drimindhu' deelish,* my darling black cow,
Say where are your folk, be they living or no?
They are down in the ground 'neath the sod, lying low,
Expecting King James with the crown on his brow.

II.

But if I could get sight of the crown on his brow,
By night and day travelling to London I'd go,
Over mountains of mist and black mosses below,
'Till I'd beat on the kettle-drums *drimindhubh O!*

III.

Welcome home, welcome home, *drimindhubh O!*
Good was your sweet-milk for drinking, I trow;
With your face like a rose, and your dewlap of snow,
I'll part from you never, my *drimindhubh O!*"

XII. (No. 46 in the Collection.) *Gráine Mhael.* "Granu Weal."—So called from Grace O'Malley, a noted Irish heroine of the time of Elizabeth, whose name in like manner was used as a metaphor for Ireland by the Jacobite party during these wars, and indeed has been so applied by the Irish generally ever since. Some very interesting particulars of the life of Grace O'Malley have been preserved, and are now so popularly known, that it is deemed unnecessary to repeat more of her history than that she was the daughter of O'Malley, of the Oules, a district in Mayo, and was successively the wife of O'Flaherty, of Iar-Connaught, and of Sir Richard Burk, styled the Mac William Eighter, who died in 1585. For the romantic particulars of her visit to Queen Elizabeth, and to Howth Castle, from which she carried off the youthful heir of the house of St. Laurence, see *Anthologia Hibernica* for the years 1793-4. The air is probably as old as the heroine whose name it bears. The Jacobite words are, however, those universally sung to it, and are superior in point of diction and sentiment to most others of the same class. When played on the pipes, the tune at intervals is made to have a peculiar sound, which has procured it the additional name of "Ma, Ma, Ma."

XIII. (No. 113 in the Collection.) *Géadha Fiadhaine.* "The Wild Geese."—The finest of this class of melodies, and the most affecting, both in its origin and in the frequent allusions made to it throughout the modern songs of the Irish. It was composed as a farewell to the gallant remnant of the Irish army, who, upon the capitulation of Limerick in 1691, preferred an honourable exile to remaining in the country when their cause was lost, and who afterwards so well sustained the national reputation, under the name of the Irish Brigade, in the Continental wars. It is commonly believed that the air was sung by the women assembled on the shore at the time of the embarkation. From the following account of that event, it would appear that the occasion was one by no means unlikely to call forth such a demonstration. "Barbarous and inhuman hath been Wahop's usage to the poor Irish, which lately were shipped from Kerry. He, finding while they lay encamped, (waiting for transport ships,) that they began to desert him upon account of the ill condition of their wives and families in this kingdom, promised to take them also with him; and a declaration to that effect having been issued by Sarsfield and Wahop, they accordingly were brought to the waterside, when Wahop, pretending to ship the soldiers in order, according to his lists of them, first carried the men on board; many of the women, at the second return of the boats for the officers, catching hold to be carried on board, were dragged off with the boats, and through fearfulness loosing their hold, were drowned; others who held faster, had their fingers cut off, and came to the same miserable end, in sight of their husbands and relations."[a] A very affecting allusion to this "flight of the wild geese" occurs in a county Cork *Caoine*, composed by a father on the death of his sons, who had been drowned at sea.

"My long grief and my loss that you had not gone on ship-board
In company with Sir James, as the wild geese have done;
Then my loving trust would be in God that I would have your company again,
And that the stormy sea should not become the marriage bed of my children."[b]

XIV. (No. 108 in the Collection.) *Baal tigh abhoran*, usually called "Baltiorum," a tune which might, perhaps, without rashness, be assigned to the Pagan period, inasmuch as it is still customarily sung at the bonfires lighted on St. John's Eve, the anniversary of the *Baal-tinne*, and has so been sung from time immemorial. If the orthography of the name, as given above, could be depended on, this joined to the fact just mentioned would be conclusive; but as "Baal tigh" has been questioned, the Editor deems it safer to notice the air in this class, leaving the inquiry as to its proper name and origin to some more able Irish scholar.

XV. (No. 101 in the Collection.) *Cara Ceann dilis.* "Black-headed Dear."—This ancient air has hitherto been improperly set in a minor, instead of a major key. A slight

[a] From the *Dublin Intelligence*, published by authority in the year 1691.

[b] The following beautiful lines on the "Wild Geese," are from the pen of a lamented friend, written many years since expressly for this work, in imitation of the Irish:

Géadha Fiadhaine, "The Wild Geese," or Ireland's Lamentation, by Dr. Drennan.

I.

"How solemn sad by Shannon's flood
The blush of morning sun appears!
To men who gave for us their blood,
Ah, what can woman give but tears?
How still the field of battle lies!
No shouts upon the breezes blown!
We heard our dying country's cries,
We sit deserted and alone.
Ogh hone, ogh hone, ogh hone, ogh hone,
Ogh hone, &c.
Ah, what can woman give but tears?

II.

Why thus collected on the strand
Whom yet the God of Mercy saves?
Will ye forsake your native land?
Will ye desert your brothers' graves?
Their graves give forth a fearful groan,
Oh guard your orphans and your wives;
Like us, make Erin's cause your own,
Like us, for her yield up your lives.
Ogh hone, ogh hone, ogh hone, ogh hone,
Ogh hone, &c.
Like us, for her yield up your lives."

examination will prove that the setting now adopted bears in itself strong marks of genuine originality. In a small collection of Irish airs, published about 1720, by Neal, of Christ Church Yard, Dublin, *Cara Ceann Dilis* is found in a minor key; and that setting has been adopted by Burke Thumoth in his "Collection of Irish Tunes," about 1725, as well as by Oswald in his "Caledonian Pocket Companion." But, as it is sung by the peasantry to this day in the style and manner given in this work, the setting here adopted is presumed to be correct. No Irish words can now be found for the air, as set in a minor key.

XVI. (No. 100 in the Collection.) *Tá me mo Chodladh.* "I am asleep, and don't waken me."—An ancient and beautiful air, unwarrantably appropriated by the Scotch, among whom Hector M'Neill has written words to it. The Irish words are evidently very old, and consist only of six lines :

"I am asleep, without rocking, through this quarter of the night;
I am asleep, and do not waken me;
O kindly, dear mother, gėt up and make light for me,
For I am sick, and evil has happened me," &c. &c.

O'Neill tells us the following curious anecdote connected with this tune. When at Mr. Macdonnell's of Knockrantry in the county of Roscommon, he met a young nobleman from Germany who had come to Ireland to look after some property to which he had a claim through his mother. "He was one of the most finished and accomplished young gentlemen," says O'Neill, "that I ever met. When on one occasion Hugh O'Neill and I had played our best tunes for him, he wished to call for "Past one o'Clock," or *Tha me mo Chodladh, naar dhoesk a me,* which he had heard played somewhere before, but for the name of which he was at a loss. Perceiving me going towards the door, he followed me, and said that the name of his bootmaker was Tommy M'Cullagh, and that the tune he wanted was like saying 'Tommy M'Cullagh made boots for me;' and in the broad way he pronounced it, it was not unlike the Irish name. I went in with him and played it, on which he seemed uncommonly happy."—(O'Neill MS.)

XVII. (No. 115 in the Collection.) *Abhran Sligighe.* "Sligo Tune."—The first bar of this ancient air is like the Scotch song, "Will you go to the Ewe boughts Marion ;" the wildness of the melody is remarkable, though not without merit.

XVIII. (No. 125 in the Collection.) *An Chuaich in mhaiseach.* "The Bonny Cuckoo."—From this ancient melody, procured by the Editor in the poetical district of Ballinascreen, another tune, "The little and great Mountain," seems to have been arranged with some slight variations. The following words to the "Bonny Cuckoo," are a close translation from the original Irish.

"My bonny Cuckoo I tell you true,
That thro' the groves I'll rove with you;
I'll rove with you until the next spring,
And then my Cuckoo shall sweetly sing.
I'll rove with you until the next spring,
And then my Cuckoo shall sweetly sing.

The ash and the hazel shall mourning say,
My bonny Cuckoo, don't go away;
Don't go away, but tarry here,
And make the season last all the year.
Don't go away, but tarry here,
And make the season last all the year."

XIX. (No. 95 in the Collection.) *Aileog bheag.* "The little Swallow."—Another charming air from Ballynascreen. The words which have been handed down by tradition are simple and appropriate to the air, commencing :

"I would I were a little swallow,
I would rise into the air and fly
Away to that inconstant rover,"
&c. &c.

"Slieve gallen," (No. 24 in the Collection,) is also a Ballinascreen air, arranged by Lyons in 1700.

XX. (No. 84 in the Collection.) *Slainte òn Chopán.* "Health from the Cup."—A pleasing memorial of the celebrated Richard Kirwan of Cregg, by whom it was presented to the Editor in the year 1792. The quaintness and brevity of the air, and the fact of its consisting of only one part, are strong arguments of a high degree of antiquity.

XXI. (No. 29 in the Collection.) *Ciste no Stór.* "Coffers nor Stores."—This very ancient air seems to have been the original of Carolan's Fairy Queen, the only difference being that Carolan has added two more parts to it, in which way it was generally played by the harpers. In an old printed copy of the Fairy Queen, published about 1725, in the Editor's possession, it is still more extended, but by being so it loses its effect. The Editor obtained this charming melody from the late Doctor Matthew Young, afterwards Bishop of Clonfert. It takes its name from the first line of the accompanying verses.

"Coffers or stores I never shall prize,
But dicing, and quaffing, and music;
For I am gone mad for the love of a maiden, and I cannot sleep," &c. &c.

XXII. (No. 126 in the Collection.) *Feaduidhil an airimh.* "The Ploughman's Whistle."—This curious melody is given in Walker's Irish Bards; but, from its being set there in common instead of triple time, it is difficult to be understood. It is given here as whistled by the ploughman, and nearly in the acute sounds of the whistler, to imitate which the tune must be played very slowly, and with the utmost expression. The second part bears a strong resemblance to the primitive air sung by the boatmen on the rivers in China; both melodies have the same cadence, and the only difference is in the time, the Chinese air being in common, the Irish in triple time. It may be observed here, that in many instances there is a remarkable coincidence between the Hindostanee airs, published by Bird, and the Irish melodies, proving the strong resemblance which exists amongst the primitive strains of all nations.

XXIII. (No. 137 in the Collection.) *Feaduidhil an airimh Condae an Righ.* "Ploughman's Whistle of King's County," is of a more plaintive character, having a very melancholy and tender expression. It is considered by the Editor to belong to the most ancient class of melodies. It may be performed an octave lower, with the best effect; but as the higher octave, in which it is set, agrees best with the shrill high sound made in whistling, it is arranged accordingly.

XXIV. (No. 18 in the Collection.) *Roisin Dubh.* "Black Rose-bud."—A term of endearment. The melody is undoubtedly very ancient.[a] It was sung for the Editor in 1792, by Daniel Black, the harper, who played chords in the Arpeggio style with excellent effect. The key-note at the end of the strain, accompanied by the fifth and eighth, without the third, has a wailing, melancholy expression, which imparts a very peculiar effect to the melody.

XXV. (No. 19 in the Collection.) *Roisin Bheag Dubh.* "Little Black Rose-bud."—Differs only slightly from the preceding. It is here set according to the version preserved in the lower glens of the county of Antrim. The cadence at the termination seems to lean so much more to E than A, that the Editor has adopted the former key-note as its tonic. This curious anomaly is frequently observed in these simple airs.

XXVI. (No. 34 in the Collection.) *Sheela ny Kelly.* "Sarah Kelly."—This air is by Thomas Connallon. Part of it is played by crossing the hands, technically called in Irish, *Malart Phonche*, and shews the degree of perfection to which the older harpers carried their performances. Carolan composed words for it.

XXVII. (No. 109 in the Collection.) *Peggi ni Leavan*, or "Bonny Portmore."—A favourite air in the country about Ballinderry, in the county of Antrim. Portmore, an old residence of the O'Neills, stood on the banks of Lough Beg, a small and shallow, but picturesque, sheet of water adjoining Loch Neagh. The ivy-clad ruins of the old church still stand on a neighbouring eminence, which in summer forms a promontory, and in winter is surrounded by the waters of the lake. On the plantation of this part of the country in 1611, Portmore became the property of Lord Conway, who built a mansion here, of which there are still some traces. This was a favourite retreat of Doctor Jeremy Taylor, when Bishop of Dromore; and the tree under which he used to sit, to hear this melody sung by the peasantry, was pointed out, until some years ago. The air is probably as old as the time of the O'Neills, of Ballinderry, to whose declining fortunes there would appear to be an allusion in the first stanza of the English words, which are still sung with it:

"Bonny Portmore, you shine where you stand,
And the more I think on you, the more my heart warms;
But if I had you now, as I had once before,
All the gold in all England would not buy you, Portmore!"

XXVIII. (No. 90 in the Collection.) *Molly Bheag O.* "Little Molly."—The undoubted original of "Molly Astore," which, however highly prized as a national air,

[a] The words are assigned by Mr. Hardiman to the period of Red Hugh O'Donnell's rebellion in the latter end of the sixteenth century, but there appear no sufficient grounds for affirming this with certainty.

must be admitted to be no more than an arrangement of this more ancient and not less characteristic melody.

XXIX. (No. 43 in the Collection.) *Bruach an Claudae.* "Banks of Claudy."—Interesting for its peculiar bass accompaniment, which was taken down from the harper nearly as it is here given.

XXX. (No. 11 in the Collection.) *Conchobhar Mac Areibhe.* "Connor Mac Areavy," known also by the name of *Calleena bhacha su Seorse,* "Girls, have you seen George ?"—The melody is extremely ancient, and the variations by Lyons (Lord Antrim's harper) are excellent. The modern musician will be surprised to find such an admirable arrangement by a person ignorant (as it is presumed all the Irish harpers at the beginning of the eighteenth century were) of modern musical science.

XXXI. (No. 38 in the Collection.) *Sin Sios agus suas liom.* "Down beside me."—Is the original of "Shepherds, I have lost my Love." It is set here as taken from the performance of Dominic Mungan, the celebrated harper, the father of Bishop Warburton.

XXXII. (No. 50 in the Collection.) *Cad fath nach n-deun-fadh na boichte.* "Why should not poor Folk ?"—Was noted down by the Editor, in the year 1792, from the performance of an old man, well known by the *soubriquet* of "Poor Folk," who formerly perambulated the northern counties, playing on a tin fiddle.

XXXIII. (No. 146 in the Collection.) *Gearrfhiad san narbhar.* "The Hare in the Corn."—An ancient tune for the pipes, in which there is an imitation of a hunt, including the sound of the huntsmen's horns, the crying of the dogs, and finally, the distress and death of the hare. This performance can only be given on the pipes, the chanter or principal tube of which, when pressed with its lower end against the leather guard on the performer's knee, can be made to yield a smothered, sobbing tone, very appropriate to the dying cry of the hare, but difficult to imitate or describe in musical notation.

XXXIV. (No. 132 in the Collection.) *Blath dubh is bhan.* "The Black and White Garland," is allied to that peculiar class of airs called *Lunigs* in Scotland, and *Loobeens* in Ireland, of which three other specimens are noticed below. It has been a favourite at the festive meetings of the peasantry from time immemorial. It is first sung by one person, and then repeated in chorus by the whole assembly. The setting given here, which is that of the air as popularly sung, seems irregular, in the transposition of the first four bars, which ought to occupy the place of the second four, and *vice versa,* to make the arrangement correspond with the model on which Irish melodies are generally constructed.

XXXV. (Nos. 134, 135, and 136, in the Collection.) *Three Loobeens.*—The Loobeen is a peculiar species of chaunt, having a very well marked time, and a frequently recurring chorus or catch-word. It is sung at merry-makings and assemblages of the young women, when they meet at "spinnings" or "quiltings," and is accompanied by extemporaneous verses, of which each singer successively furnishes a line. The intervention of the chorus after each line gives time for the preparation of the succeeding one by the next singer, and thus the *Loobeen* goes round, until the chain of song is completed. Hence its name, signifying literally the "link tune." Of course there is a great variety of words, and these usually of a ludicrous character, such as might be expected from the *crambo* verses of rustics. The airs themselves bear all the appearance of antiquity.

XXXVI. (No. 148 in the Collection.) *As fada annso me.* "Long am I here," or "The gentle Maiden," from which the air of "My lodging is on the cold ground" has been taken, is undoubtedly pure Irish, as is proved by the characteristic national tone of the sub-mediant in the fourth bar, continued at intervals through the melody.

To this class may also be referred several other melodies, concerning which the Editor has nothing further to mention beyond what will be found in the general Index.

AIRS OF THE THIRD CLASS—MODERN.

I. (No. 45 in the Collection.) *Bainphrionnsa Rioghamhuil.* "The Princess Royal." —A fine air, composed by Carolan for the daughter of Macdermott Roe, the representative of the old princes of Coolavin. It is now well known by the name of the "Arethusa," a spirited and popular sea song, and is a charming specimen of the blind bard's genius.

II. (No. 127 in the Collection.) *Plangstae Teaboid Peiton.* "Planxty Peyton."—Another of Carolan's, equally characteristic in structure and in origin. Squire Toby Peyton, of Lisduff, in the county of Leitrim, was an Irish gentleman of the old school, a sportsman, convivialist, and an ardent lover of the harp. O'Neill, in whose time he was still living, and who often enjoyed the hospitalities of Lisduff, gives this account of him: "Toby Peyton had a fine unincumbered estate, and, exclusive of the expenses of groceries and spices, spent the remainder of his income in encouraging national diversions, particularly harping and playing on all other stringed instruments. He lived to the age of 104 years, and when he was 100, would mount his horse as actively as a man of twenty, and be the first in at the death, whether it was a fox or a hare."[a] The tune had its origin in the following circumstance. The squire, meeting Carolan on horseback, said to him jocosely in Irish, "Carolan, you ride crooked," to which the harper, who was exceedingly sensitive in every thing touching his personal appearance, replied, "I'll pay you for that with a crooked tune." He, accordingly, composed this air, which is in truth of such a crabbed, unmanageable nature, as almost to defy every rule of composition in the adaptation of a bass. It answers well the description of old national airs given by Dr. Burney, who says, "We may judge of the little attention that was paid to keys by the awkward difficulties to which those are subject who attempt to clothe them with harmony."

III. (No. 107 in the Collection.) *Ineen-i-Hamilton.* "Hamilton's Daughter."—Remarkable as being the composition of the last of the old race of Irish harpers. It is a piece of Lyons's, but to what Miss Hamilton it was addressed, the Editor is not aware, though the probability is that she was one of the Killileagh family. None of the successors of Lyons attempted to compose an air; their utmost effort was a meagre attempt at arrangement.

[a] O'Neill MS.

IV. (No. 55 in the Collection.) *An Graidheair duilteach.* "The rejected Lover."—This air varies from the other melodies in the Collection, in the extreme shortness of its phrases, (nearly one in each bar.) The repetition of the note in the first and second bars at the beginning of the second part, and also at the end of the tune, is a characteristic trait in Irish music. The following words are sung to the air:

"Her hair was like the beaten gold,
Or like the spider's spinning;
It was in her you might behold
My joys and woes beginning."
&c. &c. &c.

V. (No. 124 in the Collection.) *Meinguilt mhic Seoine.* "Jackson's Morning Brush."—The work of a composer who lived later than the time of Lyons, but who did not cultivate the harp. He composed several excellent jig tunes, "Jackson's Morning Brush," "Jackson's Bottle of Punch," &c., which were remarkable for original melody and sprightliness, and answered very well for dancing, but were generally performed on the bagpipe or violin. He was for some time resident in the county of Monaghan, and, from the following passage in M'Gregor's History of Limerick, appears to have been possessed of property in that county also:

"Jackson's Turret, built on a hill, (in the parish of Ballingarry, barony of Upper Connello, and county of Limerick,) was formerly the residence of Mr. Jackson, who was celebrated for his skill on the Irish bagpipes, and the composition of some of our most admired national airs. This turret was a fine object to the surrounding country, but is now (1826) nearly in ruins, having been struck by lightning some years ago."[a]

VI. (No. 142 in the Collection.) *Cailin deas chum brathar fanich;* or,

"A lovely lass to a friar came
To confess in a morning early."

This is the only air admitted into the collection which is not of unquestionable Irish origin; but the Editor has adopted it as Irish, on the authority of all the old harpers with whom he has conversed: it was at all times a favourite tune of theirs. The emphatic manner in which the fourth tone of the scale is used, seems to claim for it a high antiquity, and justifies the restoration of the air to its proper place among the melodies of Ireland. It is a very sweet tune, and the higher and lower octaves aptly coincide with the alternations of the male and female voices in the song.

The remaining airs, which may be considered as belonging to the modern class, will be found in the Collection.

SIC TRANSIT GLORIA CITHARÆ.

[a] M'Gregor's History of Limerick, vol. i. p. 381.

THE

ANCIENT MUSIC

OF

IRELAND.

Arranged for the

PIANO FORTE.

INDEX

TO

THE IRISH NAMES OF THE AIRS,

ALPHABETICALLY ARRANGED.

NAMES IN IRISH CHARACTERS.	NAMES IN ENGLISH CHARACTERS.	TRANSLATION.	PAGE.
A muirnin,	A muirnin,	The darling,	77
Aḃran ṡligiġ,	Abhrán Sligighe,	Sligo tune,	86
Aḃrán ṡloiñ,	Abhran Shloin,	Sloan's lamentation,	87
Aeḋear ċarraic ṁic ċroise,	Aedhear Carraic mhic croise,	Carrickmacross air,	91
Aileóg ḃeag,	Aileog bheag,	The little swallow,	70
Air an m-baile so ta cuil-ḟioñ,	Air an m-baile so ta cuil-fhionn,	In this village lives a fair maid,	14
An ḃfeacaḋ tu an stuaḋaire duḃ?	An bhfeaca tu an stuadhaire dubh?	Did you see the black rogue?	4
An ḃrad-óg ḃréugaċ,	An brad-og breugach,	The cunning young girl,	18
An ċuaċ in ṁaiseaċ,	An chuaich in mhaiseach,	The bonny cuckoo,	96
An cruisgín ḃeag,	An cruiskin bheag,	The little pot,	98
An caóine, gul, caoine ḃeag, caoine mór,	An caoine, gol, caoine bheag, caoine mor,	Irish cry, lamentation, little cry, great cry,	59
An ceañaiḋe sugaċ,	An ceannaidhe sugach,	The jolly merchant,	4
An deileadóir,	An deladoir,	The wheelright,	28
An déircṫeóir,	An deirctheoir,	The beggarman,	63
An foġlaiḋe,	An foghlaidhe,	The robber, or Charley Reilly,	48
An graiḋeóir diultaḋaé,	An graidheoir duilteach,	The rejected lover,	41
An lon duḃ agus án smolaċ,	An londubh agus an smolach,	The blackbird and the thrush,	3

NAMES IN IRISH CHARACTERS.	NAMES IN ENGLISH CHARACTERS.	TRANSLATION.	PAGE.
An londuḃ agus an ċeirseaċ,	An londubh agus an cheirseach,	The blackbird and the hen,	5
An londuḃ,	An londubh,	The blackbird,	72
An luibín,	An luibhin,	The spinning wheel song,	100
An maidrín ruaḋ,	An maidrin ruadh,	The little bold fox,	98
An seanduine spad ċluasaċ,	An sean duine spad-clusach,	The deaf old man,	78
An spailpín fánaċ,	An spailpin fánach,	The girl I left behind me,	43
An toireaṁ sugaċ,	An t-oireamh súgach,	The jolly ploughman,	20
An bromaċ fiaḋain,	An bromach fiadhain,	The wild colt,	103
As fada annso me,	As fada annso me,	Long am I here, or the gentle maiden,	108
Baaltiġ aḃran,	Baaltigh abhoran,	Baaltiorum,	79
Bacaċ buiḋe na leimneaḋ,	Bacach buidhe na leimne,	The lame yellow beggar,	18
Bantiarna Iḃeaċaḋ,	Baintighearna Iveach,	Lady Iveach,	2
Bantiaġearna Blánaḋ,	Baintighearna Blaney,	Lady Blaney,	45
Bantiġearna Crofton,	Baintighearna Crofton,	Mrs. Crofton,	19
Baintiġearna Macsḃell,	Baintighearna Maxwell,	Madam Maxwell,	68
Beanṗrioñsa Rioġaṁuil,	Bainphrionnsa Rioghamhuil,	The Princess Royal,	35
Beir mo ġráḋ,	Beir mo ghradh,	Take my love to that young man,	37
Blaṫ doñ is bán,	Blath donn is bhan,	The brown and white garland,	99
Bo ṁaol,	Bo mhaol,	The hornless cow,	29
Braḃaḋ Cearḃallain,	Brabhadh Chearbhallain,	Carolan's devotion,	53
Bríġid og na gciaḃ,	Brighid og na gciabh,	Young Bridget with the fair locks,	82
Bruaċna carraige baine,	Bruach na carraige báine,	The bank of the white rocks,	22
Bruaċ an Chlaudaiġ,	Bruach an Claudaigh,	Banks of Claudy,	33
Buaileam treal ċum tseoil,	Buaileam tréal chum tseoil,	Preparing to sail,	25
Bunnán buiḋe,	Bunnan buidhe,	The yellow bittern,	56
Cailin deas ċum braṫar tainic,	Cailin deas chum brathar tainic,	A lovely lass to a friar came,	104
Cailin na gruaige duiḃe,	Cailin na gruaige duibhe,	The black-haired girl,	25
Cad faṫ naċ ndéunfaḋ na boiċt?	Cad foth nach n-deunfadh na boicht?	Why should not poor folk?	38

NAMES IN IRISH CHARACTERS.	NAMES IN ENGLISH CHARACTERS.	TRANSLATION.	PAGE.
Cailín deas ruaḋ, . . .	Caillin deas ruadh, . . .	The pretty red girl, . .	66
Caitlín ní Chuin̄, . . .	Cait ni Chuinn, ...	Kitty Quin, ...	66
Cáit ní Nualain, . . .	Cait ni Nualain, ...	Kitty Nowlan, ...	71
Caitlín ni Aġra, . . .	Caitlin ni Eaghra, . . .	Kitty O'Hara, ...	30
Caillin deas don̄, . . .	Callin deas donn, ...	The pretty brown maid, .	40
Caṫal Mac Aoḋa, . . .	Cathal Mhac Aodha, . .	Charles Machugh the wild boy, ...	50
Cara ċean̄ dilis, . . .	Cara ceann dilis, ...	Black-headed deary, . .	75
Ciste sa stór, ...	Ciste sa stor, ...	My love and treasure, .	24
Clara a Ḃurc, ...	Clara a Burc, ...	Clara Burk, ...	73
Cnoc na coille, ...	Cnoc na coille, ...	The woodhill, or Lady Maisterton, ...	8
Conċoḃar Macareiḃe, .	Conchobhar Macareibhe, .	Connor Macareavy, . .	10
Contae Ṫhir Eoġain, . .	Contae Tir Eoghain, . .	County Tyrone, . . .	97
Cupán ni Ara, ...	Copan ni Eaghra, . . .	Doctor John Hart, . .	23
Cran̄ ar an ċoill, . . .	Crann air an choill, . . .	The tree in the wood, .	40
Cronán, ...	Cronán, ...	Ballinderry and Cronan, .	42
Cúan milis an ċallaiḋ, .	Cuan milis an challaidh, .	Sweet Portaferry, . . .	55
Cuilin̄, ...	Cuilin, ...	Coolin, ...	88
Cuṁa an deiḃin̄si, . . .	Cumha an deibhinnsi, . .	The lamentation of youths,	92
Cuṁa caoine an Albanaiġ,	Cumha caoine an Albanaigh,	Scotts' lamentation, . .	6
Cuma Mic Ġuiḋir, . . .	Cumha Mheg Guidhir, . .	Maguire's lamentation, .	28
Daṁsa loin̄eaċ, ...	Daimsa loineach, ...	Chorus jig, ...	76
Da mbeiḋ cuirt agam is caislean̄, ...	Da mbeidh cuirt agam is caisleamh, ...	If I had a court and castle,	99
Diarmuid agus a ċailín, .	Dearmid agus a cailin, . .	Dermott and his lass, . .	65
Do bi bean uasal, . . .	Do bhe bean uasal, ...	There was a young lady,	52
Drinmin duḃ, ...	Druimin dubh, ...	Dear black cow, . . .	32
Druċt an ċeo, ...	Drucht an cheo, ...	The foggy dew, . . .	109
Eiḃlin a Ruin̄, ...	Eibhlin a Ruin, ...	Ellen a Roone, . . .	94
Eamon Doḋball, . . .	Emon Dabhal, ...	Emon Dodwell, . . .	77
Faire! faire! ar aġaiḋ ar aġaiḋ, ...	Faire! faire! ar aghaidh ar aghaidh, ...	Watch, watch, advance, advance. The Pharroh, or war march, . . .	105
Fannuiḋ Pouer, ...	Fannuidh Power, ...	Fanny Power, ...	49

NAMES IN IRISH CHARACTERS.	NAMES IN ENGLISH CHARACTERS.	TRANSLATION.	PAGE.
Feaduiḋil an aiṙiṁ,	Feaduidhil an airimh,	The ploughman's whistle,	101
Feaduiḋil an aiṙiṁ Condae an Riġ,	Feaduidhil an airimh Condae an Righ,	The ploughman's whistle, King's County,	96
Fiaċa ui ḃúrc,	Fiacha a Burc,	Sir Festus Burk,	34
Fiġimse lín is olan̄,	Fighim-se lin a's ollann,	I can weave linen and woollen,	44
Fonn aiċle,	Fonn aichile,	Achill tune,	106
Fonn an aḃranaiḋ,	Fonn an abhranaidh,	The chanter's tune,	107
Fonn ċille camniġ,	Fonn cille camnigh,	Kilkenny tune,	108
Gaṁna geala,	Gamhna geala,	The white calves,	41
Geaḋa fiaḋaiṅe,	Geadha fiadhaine,	The wild geese,	84
Gráine ṁael,	Gráine mhael,	Granu weal, or ma, ma, ma,	36
Gearrḟiaḋ san narḃar,	Gearrfhiadh san narbhar,	The hare in the corn,	107
huis an cat,	Huis an cat,	Hush the cat,	3
Inġean̄ an toiciġ ⁊ an mairnealaċ,	Inghean an toicigh gus an mairnealach,	A sailor and a farmer's daughter,	102
Is buaċaill goiḋaisteaċ mé,	Is buachaill goidisteach me,	I am a poor rambling boy,	71
Is iasgaire Locca ar Céara mé,	Is iásgaire ar Locha Ceara me,	I am a fisherman on Lough Carra,	68
Is galar cráite an gráḋ,	Is galarcraiohte an gradh,	Love's a tormenting pain,	44
Lá ḟéile Paidric,	La feile Paidric,	Patrick's day,	67
Maiḋinn doṁnaigh,	Maidinn domhnaigh,	Sunday morning,	15
Maiḋin ḃog áoiḃin,	Maidin bhog avibhinn,	Soft mild morning,	57
Maire óg na gciaḃ,	Maire óg nā gciabh,	Mary with the fair locks,	49
Mairseál ni Dhoṁnaill,	Mairseail ni Dhomhnaill,	O'Donnell's march,	58
Mairsail Alisḋrum,	Mairseail alasdroim,	Macdonnell's march,	83
Maire a stór,	Molly astor,	Mary, my treasure,	46
Máire ḃeag O!	Molly bheag O,	Little Molly O,	67
Mianairea cille meanntain,	Mianairea cille meanntain,	The miners of Wicklow,	76
Muirguilt ṁicseoin̄,	Muis-guilt mhic seoin,	Jackson's morning brush,	95
Nead na cuaiċe,	Nead na cuaiche,	The cuckoo's nest,	81

INDEX TO THE IRISH NAMES OF THE AIRS.

NAMES IN IRISH CHARACTERS.	NAMES IN ENGLISH CHARACTERS.	TRANSLATION.	PAGE.
Nañiuḋ hamultún,	Neeni Hamilton,	Miss Hamilton,	79
Ní mian liom,	Ni mian liom,	I do not incline,	65
Noinin Choñaċtaċ,	Noinin Conachtach,	The Connaught daisy,	85
Noirín mo ṁile stoirín,	Noirin mo mhile stoirin,	Nora, my thousand treasures,	24
O! Maeḃi ġeal O!	O! Maebhi gheal O!	O! white Maive,	102
O! Maire ḋilis,	O! Maire deelish,	O! Molly dear,	87
Onora an ċisde,	Onora an chisde,	Nora with the cake,	22
Paidín na Raiḃeartaiġ,	Paidin O'Raibheartaigh,	Paddy O'Rafferty,	64
Peggi ni labaiñ,	Peggi ni leavan,	Bonny Portmore,	80
Planxtae Aoḋa Mic Doṁneil,	Plangstigh Aodha Mhic Domhneil,	Planxty Hugh O'Donnell,	47
Plancstae Sealuis Cuta,	Plangstigh Charles Coote,	Planxty Charles Coote,	26
Plangstae Ḃhuairciḋ,	Plangstigh Burke,	Planxty Burk,	31
Planxtae Teaboid Peiton,	Plangstigh Toby Peyton,	Planxty Toby Peyton,	97
Planxtae inġeañ ni Ḃhuairċiḋ,	Plangstigh ingheann ni Bherairchidh,	Planxty Miss Burk,	43
Raiñce gaoḋalaċ,	Rainnce gaodhalach,	Irish jig,	109
Raiñce piobare,	Rainnce piobare,	Piper's dance,	36
Receipt ui Chearḃallaiñ,	Receipt ui Chearbhallain,	Carolan's receipt,	54
Roisin duḃ,	Roisin dubh,	Black rose bud,	16
Roisin ḃeag ḋuḃ,	Roisin bheag dubh,	Little black rose bud,	17
Roisin ní Choñillain,	Roisin Connolly,	Rose Connolly,	14
Ros gan ruḃa,	Rós gan rubha,	The rose without rue,	12
Sagart'ne an sagart?	Sagart'né an sagart?	Is it the priest you want?	86
Seaḃac na heirne,	Seabhac na h-Eirne,	The hawk of Ballyshannon,	13
Seumus óg,	Séamus óg Plunket,	Young James Plunket,	26
Séumus a ċaca a ċaill eire,	Seamus a chaca a chaill eire,	Dirty James, that lost Ireland,	50
Síola ní Ceallinḋ,	Sheela ni Kelly,	Saely Kelly,	27
Sile ni Choiñallam,	Sile ni Chonnallain,	Celia Connallon,	37
Sheela beg ní Choñallaiñ,	Sheela beg ni Chonnallain,	Celia Connallon, second set,	91
Sín sios agus suas liom,	Sin sios agus suas liom,	Down beside me,	30
Slainte án ċupan,	Slainte an chupain,	Health from the cup,	64

NAMES IN IRISH CHARACTERS.	NAMES IN ENGLISH CHARACTERS.	TRANSLATION.	PAGE.
Sliaḃ Guilleaṅ,	Slieve Gallen,	Slieve Gallen,	21
Suiḋ sios ar mo ḋiḋion,	Suidh shios ar mo dhidion,	Sit down under my protection,	1
Suisín ban,	Suisin ban,	The white blanket,	51
Suisin buiḋe,	Suisin buidhe,	The yellow blanket,	58
Taḃar ḋam do laṁ,	Tabhair dam do lamh,	Give me your hand,	46
Ta me mo ċodlaḋ,	Ta me'mo chodladh,	I am asleep, and don't waken me,	74
Ta me a neuġṁais ac ioċḟaiḋ ṁe ḟás,	Ta me a neighmais ac iocfaidh mhe fas,	I'm in debt, but I'll pay them yet,	103
Tarraing go caoin an sgéul,	Tarraing go caoin an sgol,	Consider the story,	54
Tír ḟiaċraiċ,	Tir fhiachrach,	Tyreragh,	31
Triall an iománaiġ,	Triall an jomanaigh,	The hurler's march,	99
Truaġ naċ ḃfaicim mo ġráḋ,	Truagh nach bfaicim mo gradh,	'Tis a pity I don't see my love,	69
Tu féin 'sme féin,	Tu fein sme fein,	Yourself along with me,	16
Tuireaṁ ui Raġallaiġ,	Tuireamh in Raghallaigh,	O'Reilly's lament,	106
Uair ḃeag roiṁ lá,	Uair bheag roimh lá,	A little hour before day,	48
Uċ nan uaċ is osna lar mo cleiḃ,	Uch nan uach is osna lar mo cleibh,	Alas! the pain is in my heart,	9
Uṁaiḋe Chonga, no beanan fir ruaiḋ	Umhaidhe Chonga, no banin fir ruadh,	The caves of Cong, or red man's wife,	63
Youġall duisi,	Youghall duishe,	Get up early,	39

INDEX

TO

THE ENGLISH NAMES OF THE AIRS,

ALPHABETICALLY ARRANGED.

NAME.	PAGE.	AUTHOR AND DATE.	WHERE AND FROM WHOM PROCURED.	
Achill air, ...	106	Very ancient, author and date unknown,	George Petrie, Esq. A.D.	1839
Alas! the pain is in my heart,	9	Very ancient, author and date unknown,	Byrne, the harper, . . .	1792
A little hour before day, . .	48	Very ancient, author and date unknown,	Byrne, the harper, . . .	1806
A lovely lass to a friar came,	104	Very ancient, author and date unknown,	Hempson, at Magilligan, .	1796
A sailor loved a farmer's daughter, ...	102	Very ancient, author and date unknown,	G. Petrie, Esq., Dublin, .	1839
Ballinderry and Cronan, . .	42	Very ancient, author and date unknown,	Doctor Crawford, Lisburn,	1808
Baltiorum, ...	79	Author and date unknown, ...	T. Conlan, ...	1831
Banks of Claudy, ...	33	Very ancient, author and date unknown,	H. Higgins, harper, . .	1792
Black rose bud, ...	16	Very ancient, author and date unknown,	D. Black, harper, . . .	1796
Black rose bud, second set, .	17	Very ancient, author and date unknown,	A peasant at Cushendall, .	1804
Black-headed deary, . . .	75	Very ancient, author and date unknown,	T. Conlan, ...	1802
Bonny Portmore, ...	80	Very ancient, author and date unknown,	D. Black, harper, at Glenoak,	1796
Carolan's devotion, ...	53	Carolan, 1690, ...	H. Higgins, harper, . .	1792
Carolan's receipt, ...	54	Carolan, ...	D. Black, harper, . . .	1796
Carrickmacross air, ...	91	Very ancient, author and date unknown,	An old woman, at Dundalk,	1794
Celia Connallon, ...	37	Thomas Connallon, 1660, ...	A. O'Neill, harper, . . .	1792
Celia Connallon, second set, .	91	Thomas Connallon, ...	Byrne, harper, ...	1792
Charles Machugh, the wild boy,	50	Very ancient, author and date unknown,	Byrne, harper, ...	1792
Chorus jig, ...	76	Author and date unknown, ...	Macdonnell, the piper, .	1797
Clara Burke, ...	73	Very ancient, author and date unknown,	Mrs. Burke, Carrakeel, County Mayo, . . .	1792
Connor Macareavy, . . .	10	Very ancient, author and date unknown, with variations by Lyons in 1700, . .	Hempson, at Magilligan, .	1792

NAME.	PAGE.	AUTHOR AND DATE.	WHERE AND FROM WHOM PROCURED.	
Consider the story, ...	54	Author and date unknown, ...	At Tipperary, . .	A.D. 1797
Coolin, or Lady of the desert,	88	Very ancient, with variations by Lyons in 1700, ...	Hempson, at Magilligan, .	1796
Dear black cow, ...	32	Very ancient, author and date unknown,	A. O'Neill, harper, . . .	1800
Dermot and his lass, . . .	65	Very ancient, author and date unknown,	H. Joy, Esq.	1800
Did you see the black rogue?	4	Very ancient, author and date unknown,	H. Higgins, harper, . .	1792
Dirty James, that lost Ireland,	50	Author and date unknown, ...	Byrne, harper, ...	1806
Doctor John Hart, ...	23	Carolan, ...	H. Higgins, harper, . .	1792
Down beside me, ...	30	Very ancient, author and date unknown,	D. Black, harper, . . .	1796
Ellen a Roone, ...	94	Very ancient, author and date unknown,	Hempson, at Magilligan, .	1792
Emon Dodwell, ...	77	Carolan, ...	C. Byrne, harper, . . .	1792
Fanny Power, ...	49	Carolan, ...	A. O'Neill, harper, . . .	1800
Get up early, ...	39	Very ancient, author and date unknown,	R. Stanton, Westport, .	1802
Give me your hand, . . .	46	O'Caghan, 1603, ...	A. O'Neill, harper, . . .	1806
Granu weal, or ma, ma, ma, .	36	Very ancient, author and date unknown,	Macdonnell, the piper, .	1797
Health from the cup, . . .	64	Very ancient, author and date unknown,	Richard Kirwan, Esq. . .	1792
Huish the cat, ...	3	Very ancient, author and date unknown,	Byrne, the harper, . . .	1802
I am a fisherman on Lough Carra, ...	68	Very ancient, author and date unknown,	Mrs. Burke, Carrakeel, County Mayo, . . .	1792
I am a poor rambling boy, .	71	Very ancient, author and date unknown,	W. Sloane, Esq., Belfast, .	1799
I am asleep, and don't waken me, ...	74	Very ancient, author and date unknown,	Hempson, harper, Magilligan, ...	1792
I can weave linen and woollen,	44	Author and date unknown, ...	J. M'Cracken, Esq., Belfast, ...	1800
I do not incline, ...	65	Author and date unknown, ...	J. M'Cracken, Esq., Belfast, ...	1810
If I had a court and castle, .	99	Author and date unknown, ...	Miss Murphy, Dublin, . .	1839
In this village lives a fair maid,	14	Very ancient, author and date unknown,	At Deel Castle, Ballina, .	1792
Irish cry, ...	59	Very ancient, author and date unknown,	O'Neill, harper, and from the hired mourners or keeners at Armagh; and from a MS. above 100 years old, ...	1799
Irish jig, ...	109	Very ancient, author and date unknown,	Macauley, Ballymoney, .	1793
Is it the priest you want? .	86	Very ancient, author and date unknown,	At Ballinrobe, ...	1792
I will pay them yet, . . .	103	Author and date unknown, ...	Mrs. B. Oranmore, County Galway, ...	1839
Jackson's morning brush, . .	95	Jackson, county Monaghan, in 1775, .	A piper, ...	1797
Kilkenny tune, ...	108	Author and date unknown, ...	E. Shannon, Esq., Dublin,	1839

NAME.	PAGE.	AUTHOR AND DATE.	WHERE AND FROM WHOM PROCURED.	
Kitty O'Hara,	30	Very ancient, author and date unknown,	At Castlebar, . . . A.D.	1802
Kitty Quin,	66	Very ancient, author and date unknown,	Byrne, harper,	1802
Kitty Nowlan,	71	Very ancient, author and date unknown,	Byrne, harper,	1806
Lady Blaney,	45	Carolan,	C. Fannin, harper,	1792
Lady Iveagh,	2	Thomas Connallon, 1660,	O'Neill, harper,	1792
Little Molly O,	67	Very ancient, author and date unknown,	C. Fannin, harper,	1792
Love's a tormenting pain,	44	William Connallon, 1670,	Hempson, at Magilligan,	1796
Madam Maxwell,	68	Carolan, about 1695,	C. Fannin, harper,	1792
Maguire's lamentation,	28	Very ancient, author and date unknown,	C. Martin, harper, Virginia, County Cavan,	1796
Mary with the fair locks,	49	Very ancient, author and date unknown,	At Deel Castle, Ballina,	1792
Macdonnell's march,	83	Author and date unknown,	A piper, at Westport,	1802
Miss Hamilton,	79	C. Lyons, harper to the Earl of Antrim, in 1702,	Patrick Linden, harper,	1802
Molly, my treasure,	46	Author and date unknown,	C. Fannin, harper,	1792
Mrs. Crofton,	19	Carolan,	C. Fannin, harper,	1792
My love and treasure,	24	Very ancient, author and date unknown,	Dr. Young, Bishop of Clonfert, at Castlereagh, County Roscommon,	1800
Nora with the purse,	22	Very ancient, author and date unknown,	Byrne, harper,	1802
Nora, my thousand treasures,	24	Very ancient, author and date unknown,	At Galway,	1802
O'Donnell's march,	58	Very ancient, author and date unknown,	R. Stanton, Westport,	1803
O! Molly dear,	87	Very ancient, author and date unknown,	Patrick Quin, harper,	1800
O'Reilly's lamentation,	106	Very ancient, author and date unknown,	J. O'Reilly, Esq., Belfast,	1806
O! white Maive,	102	Very ancient, author and date unknown,	Kitty Doo, at Armagh,	1780
Paddy O'Rafferty,	64	Author and date unknown,	J. M'Calley, at Ballymoney,	1795
Patrick's day,	67	Author and date unknown,	Patrick Quin, harper,	1792
Planxty Charles Coote,	26	Carolan,	Rose Mooney, harper,	1800
Planxty Burke,	31	Carolan,	Byrne, harper,	1802
Planxty Miss Burke,	43	Carolan,	A. O'Neill, harper,	1800
Planxty Hugh O'Donnell,	47	Carolan,	Byrne, harper,	1792
Planxty Toby Peyton,	97	Carolan,	H. Higgins, harper,	1792
Ploughman's whistle, Queen's County,	96	Very ancient, author and date unknown,	G. Petrie, Esq., Dublin,	1839
Ploughman's whistle,	101	Very ancient, author and date unknown,	Byrne, harper,	1803
Preparing to sail,	25	Very ancient, author and date unknown,	At Ballinrobe,	1792
Pretty Brown maid,	40	Very ancient, author and date unknown,	Deel Castle, Ballina,	1792
Piper's dance,	36	Very ancient, author and date unknown,	Macdonnell, piper,	1797
Rose Connolly,	14	Author and date unknown,	Coleraine,	1811

NAME.	PAGE.	AUTHOR AND DATE.	WHERE AND FROM WHOM PROCURED.	
Saely Kelly,	27	Thomas Connallon, 1660,	P. Linden, at New Town Hamilton, County Armagh, A.D.	1802
Scott's lamentation for the Baron of Loughmoe,	6	John Scott, 1599,	Hempson, harper, Magilligan,	1792
Sir Festus Burke,	34	Carolan,	C. Fannin, harper,	1792
Sit down under my protection,	1	Very ancient, author and date unknown,	Byrne, harper,	1799
Slieve Gallen,	21	Very ancient, author and date unknown,	Higgins, harper, County Roscommon,	1792
Sligo tune,	86	Very ancient, author and date unknown,	An old woman in Sligo,	1802
Sloane's lamentation,	87	Very ancient, author and date unknown,	W. Sloane, Esq., Armagh,	1800
Soft mild morning,	57	Very ancient, author and date unknown,	Hempson, Magilligan,	1796
Spinning-wheel songs,	100	Very ancient, author and date unknown,	Miss Murphy, Dublin,	1839
Sunday morning,	15	Very ancient, author and date unknown,	Redmond Stanton, at Westport,	1802
Sweet Portaferry,	55	Very ancient, author and date unknown,	J. M'Cracken, Esq., Belfast,	1800
Take my love,	37	Author and date unknown,	J. M'Cracken, Esq., Moneymore,	1802
The beggarman,	63	Author and date unknown,	G. Petrie, Esq.	1839
The blackbird and the thrush,	3	Very ancient, author and date unknown,	At Ballinrobe, County Mayo,	1792
The blackbird and the hen,	5	Very ancient, author and date unknown,	At Ballinrobe,	1792
The black-haired girl,	25	Very ancient, author and date unknown,	G. Petrie, Esq.	1822
The blackbird,	72	Very ancient, author and date unknown,	D. O'Donnell, harper, County Mayo,	1803
The bonny cuckoo,	96	Very ancient, author and date unknown,	At Ballinascreen, and from the late H. Joy, Esq., Belfast,	1793
The brink of the white rocks,	22	Very ancient, author and date unknown,	A blind man, at Westport,	1802
The brown and white garland,	99	Very ancient, author and date unknown,	G. Petrie, Esq., Dublin,	1839
The red man's wife,	63	Author and date unknown,	G. Petrie, Esq.	1839
The chanter's tune,	107	Author and date unknown,	E. Shannon, Esq.	1839
The Connaught daisy,	85	Very ancient, author and date unknown,	H. Higgins, harper,	1792
The County Tyrone,	97	Author and date unknown,	J. M'Cracken, Esq., Belfast,	1800
The cuckoo's nest,	81	Very ancient, author and date unknown,	An old music book of 1723.	
The cunning young girl,	18	Very ancient, author and date unknown,	D. O'Donnell, harper, County Mayo,	1810
The darling,	77	Very ancient, author and date unknown,	Hempson, Magilligan,	1796
The deaf old man,	78	Very ancient, author and date unknown,	Mrs. Fitzgerald, Westport,	1802
The foggy dew,	109	Very anci . t, author and date unknown,	J. McKneight, Esq., Belfast,	1839
The girl I left behind me,	43	Author and date unknown,	A. O'Neil, harper,	1800
The hare in the corn,	107	Author and date unknown,	A piper,	1800
The hawk of Ballyshannon,	13	Attributed to O'Caghan, in 1605,	A. O'Neill, harper,	1792
The hornless cow,	29	Very ancient, author and date unknown,	T. Conlan,	1833

NAME.	PAGE.	AUTHOR AND DATE.	WHERE AND FROM WHOM PROCURED.
The hurler's march, King's County,	99	Very ancient, author and date unknown,	G. Petrie, Esq., Dublin, A.D. 1839
The jolly ploughman,	20	Very ancient, author and date unknown,	J. Duncan, harper, 1792
The lame yellow beggar,	18	O'Cahan, 1640,	D. Black, harper, 1792
The lamentation of youths,	92	Harry Scott, about 1603,	D. O'Donnell, harper, at Foxford, 1802
The little swallow,	70	Very ancient, author and date unknown,	At Ballynascreen, County Derry, 1803
The little bold fox,	98	Very ancient, author and date unknown,	G. Petrie, Esq., Dublin, 1839
The little pot,	98	Author and date unknown,	Miss Murphy, Dublin, 1839
The gentle maiden,	108	Very ancient, author and date unknown,	Miss Murphy, Dublin, 1839
The jolly merchant,	4	Very ancient, author and date unknown,	C. Martin, harper, County Cavan, 1802
The miners of Wicklow,	76	Author and date unknown,	Macdonnell, piper, 1797
The Pharrah, or war march,	105	Very ancient, author and date unknown,	G. Petrie, Esq., Dublin, 1835
The pretty red girl,	66	Very ancient, author and date unknown,	Thomas Broadwood, Esq., collected in Munster, 1815
The Princess Royal,	35	Carolan,	A. O'Neill, harper, 1800
The rejected lover,	41	Author and date unknown,	Doctor W. Stokes, Dublin, 1792
The robber or Charley Reilly,	48	Very ancient, author and date unknown,	At Drogheda, 1803
The rose without rue,	12	Author and date unknown,	At Coleraine, 1810
The tree in the wood,	40	Very ancient, author and date unknown,	R. Stanton, Westport, 1802
The wheelwright,	28	Very ancient, author and date unknown,	P. Lynch, Castlebar, 1803
The white calves,	41	Very ancient, author and date unknown,	At Deel Castle, Ballina, 1792
The white blanket,	51	Very ancient, author and date unknown,	At Deel Castle, Ballina, 1792
The wild geese,	84	Very ancient, author and date unknown,	P. Quin, harper, 1803
The wild colt,	103	Author and date unknown,	G. Petrie, Esq., 1839
The woodhill, or Lady Maisterton,	8	Author and date unknown,	C. Martin, harper, at Virginia, 1800
There was a young lady,	52	Very ancient, author and date unknown,	R. Stanton, Westport, 1802
The yellow bittern,	56	Very ancient, author and date unknown,	A blind man, at Westport, 1802
The yellow blanket,	58	Very ancient, author and date unknown,	P. Quin, harper, 1806
'Tis a pity I don't see my love,	69	Very ancient, author and date unknown,	Mrs. Fitzgerald, at Westport, 1802
Tyreragh,	31	Very ancient, author and date unknown,	An old man, at Sligo, 1802
Why should not poor folk?	38	Author and date unknown,	An old man called "Poor Folk," 1807
Young Bridget,	82	Very ancient, author and date unknown,	An old man at Deel Castle, 1792
Young James Plunket,	26	Author and date unknown,	Duncan, harper, 1792
Yourself along with me,	16	Very ancient, author and date unknown,	M'Dermott, at Castlebar, 1802

SIT DOWN UNDER MY PROTECTION.

1.

By Maelzel ♩ = 104. or Pendulum 11 Inches. Very Ancient, Author and date unknown.

LADY IVEACH.

2.
Mael: ♪ = 160 — Pen: 4 Inches.
THO^S CONNALLON, 1660.
Quick and Spirited.
Cres°
Dim°

THE BLACKBIRD AND THE THRUSH.
Mael: = 108 — Pen: 10 Inches.
3.
Very Ancient, Author and date unknown.
Quick.
p
pp
HUISH THE CAT.
Mael: = 100 — Pen: 12 Inches.
4.
Author and date unknown.
Quick.
f
p

THE MERCHANT'S DAUGHTER.

Mael: ♩ = 80 — Pen 20 Inches. 5. Very Ancient, Author and date unknown.

DID YOU SEE THE BLACK ROGUE.

Mael: ♩. = 84 — Pen: 18 Inches. 6. Very Ancient, Author and date unknown.

ff
THE BLACKBIRD AND THE HEN.
Mael: = 152 — Pen: 5 Inches.
7.
Very Ancient, Author and date unknown.
In moderate time.
f
p
ff

SCOTT'S LAMENTATION FOR THE BARON OF LOUGHMOE.

Maelz. ♩ = 120 — Pen 8 Inches. 8. In 1599.

pp.
p
f
ff
Ped:
*
ff
p
f
ff
Ped:
*

THE WOOD HILL or LADY MAISTERTON.

Mael: ♪ = 108 — Pen: 10 Inches. 9. Author and date unknown.

Brisk and Lively.

ALAS! THE PAIN IS IN MY HEART.

CONNOR MACAREAVY.

11.

Mael: ♪ = 80 — Pen: 22 Inches.

Very Ancient, Author and date unknown.
Var: by LYONS in 1700.

p
f
p
Mael: ♪ = 160 — Pen: 4 Inches.
VAR: 2d
With
Spirit.
Slower
Slower

VAR: 3d
Same time as the first air.
f
ten:
Dim:
ten:
ff
ppp
THE ROSE WITHOUT RUE.
Mael: ♪ = 100 — Pen: 12 Inches.
12.
Author and date unknown.
Gracefully and lively.

THE HAWK OF BALLYSHANNON

13.

Mael: ♪ = 138 — Pen: 7 Inches. RORY DAL O' CAGHAN in 1640.

ROSE CONNOLLY.
Mael: ♩. = 88 — Pen: 16 Inches.
14.
Author and date unknown.
A little Quick.
Dim:
IN THIS VILLAGE THERE LIVES A FAIR MAID.
Mael: ♩ = 100 — Pen: 12 Inches.
15.
Very Ancient, Author and date unknown.
Gracefully and animated.
Bass very piano all through.
ff
Dim:
p
Cres:
ff

Dim:
p
pp
Cres:
ff
Dim:
p
SUNDAY MORNING.
Mael: = 120 — Pen: 8 Inches.
16.
Very Ancient, Author and date unknown.
Distinctly
and
Spirited.
f
1st time.
2nd time.
f
tr

YOURSELF ALONG WITH ME.
Mael: ♪ = 108 — Pen: 10 Inches.
17.
Very Ancient, Author and date unknown.
Quick and spirited.
p
f
BLACK ROSE BUD.
Mael: ♩ = 88 — Pen: 16 Inches.
18.
Very Ancient, Author and date unknown.
A little slow.
Ped:
The Arpeggios as originally played by the Harpers.

Ped:
Ped:
SECOND SET OF BLACK ROSE BUD.
Mael: ♩ = 88 — Pen: 16 Inches.
19.
Very Ancient, Author & date unknown.
Rather Slow.
p

THE LAME YELLOW BEGGAR.
Maelz ♪ = 104 — Pen: 11 Inches.
20.
By O'CAGHAN in 1650.
Quick but not too fast.
sf
Dol:
ff
Dim:
p
Cres:
THE CUNNING YOUNG GIRL.
Maelz ♪ = 100 — Pen: 12 Inches.
21.
Very Ancient, Author and date unknown.
Distinctly and Plaintive.
pp
f
p
Very soft

Mrs. CROFTON.

22.

Mael: ♩ = 138 — Pen: 7 Inches.

By CAROLAN.

THE JOLLY PLOUGHMAN.
Mael: ♩. = 100 — Pen: 12 Inches.
23
Very Ancient, Author and date unknown.
Brisk and Lively.
'Twas JACK the Jol-ly Plough-boy, was plough-ing in his land Cried yough un-to his hor-ses and bold-ly bid them stand.
Dolce
Then JACK sat down up-on his plough and thus be-gan to sing And JACK he sung his song so sweet he made the val-lies ring With his
CHORUS.
Too-ran-nan nan-ty na........... sing Too-ran-nan nan-ty na........... sing
Too-ran-nan Too-ran-nan Too-ran-nan Too-ran-nan Too-ran-nan nan-ty na......

SLIEVE GALLEN.

Mael: ♪ = 120 — Pen: 8 Inches. 24. Very Ancient, Author and date unknown.

NORA, WITH THE PURSE.

Mael: ♩. = 100. — Pen: 12 Inches. 25. Very Ancient, Author and date unknown.

Quick.

THE BRINK OF THE WHITE ROCKS.

Mael: ♩. = 72 — Pen: 24 Inches. 26. Very Ancient, Author and date unknown.

Slow and Tenderly.

DOCTOR JOHN HART.

Mael: ♩ = 88 — Pen: 16 Inches. 27. By CAROLAN.

NORA MY THOUSAND TREASURES.
Maels 𝅘𝅥𝅮 = 100 — Pen: 12 Inches.
28.
Very Ancient Author and date unknown.
Slow and in a singing manner.
p
Very soft
MY LOVE AND TREASURE.
Maels 𝅘𝅥𝅮 = 100 — Pen: 12 Inches.
29.
Very Ancient Author and date unknown.
In a tender animated Style.
tr
ff
pp
f
p
ppp

PREPARING TO SAIL AWAY.
Mael: ♪ = 188 — Pen: 7 Inches.
30.
Very Ancient, Author and date unknown.
Distinctly and Moderately.
THE BLACK HAIRED GIRL.
Mael: ♪ = 152 — Pen: 6 Inches.
31.
Very Ancient, Author and date unknown.
Lively and Animated.

YOUNG JAMES PLUNKET.
Mael: 𝄾 = 80 — Pen: 20 Inches.
32.
Author and date unknown
Quick and Lively.
f
p
PLANGSTY CHARLES COOTE.
Mael: 𝄾 = 108 — Pen. 10 Inches.
33.
By CAROLAN.
Very Quick and Sprightly.
sf
p
f
p

SAELY KELLY.

34.

Mael: ♪ = 92 . Pen: 15 Inches.

By THOS. CONNALLON about 1660.

THE WHEELWRIGHT.

THE HORNLESS COW.

Mael: ♩. = 96: — Pen: 13 Inches. **37.** Very Ancient, Author and date unknown.

With spirit.

pp

ff

p

Bass very soft.

DOWN BESIDE ME.
Mael: ♪ = 120 — Pen: 8 Inches.
38.
Very Ancient, Author and date unknown.
Rather Slow.
f
pp
f
KITTY O' HARA
Mael: ♩ = 88 — Pen 16 Inches:
39.
Very Ancient, Author and date unknown.
Distinctly and Moderately Quick.
f
pp
ppp
f
p

TYRERAGH.

40.

Mael: 𝅘𝅥. = 96 — Pen: 14 Inches.

Very Ancient, Author and date unknown.

Rather lively and moderate.

PLANGSTY BURKE.

41.

Mael: 𝅘𝅥. = 120 — Pen: 8 Inches.

By CAROLAN.

Very Quick.

DEAR BLACK COW.

Mael: ♪ = 88 — Pen: 16 Inches. **42.** Very Ancient, Author and date unknown.

The poor Irishman's Lamentation for the loss of his Cow.

(Translation of the Irish words.)

As I went out on a Sunday Morning
I found my Drimmin du + drowned in a moss hole
I clapp'd my hands and gave a great shout
In hopes this would bring my Drimmin du to life again
Oru Drimmin du — Oru Gra
O my Drimmin du — Lovely and fair
Oru Drimmin du — Oru Gra
O my dear Drimmin du — farewell.
There never went a spanshel upon the foot
Of a Cow that so much resembled the Glass ⁕
She had the most milk and of the sweetest taste
My grief, my mourning distress I cannot redress.
Oru Drimmin du — &c. &c. &c.

+ Drimmin dubh — i.e. Black back.

⁕ Glass Drimmin, i.e. Grey back. This was the name of a very remarkable Cow, spoken of in old stories. called also "Glass Gaivlin." she belonged to a Blacksmith, there is a hill also called "Glass Droman," and another called "Drum Gaivlin."

BANKS OF CLAUDY.

43.

Mael: ♪ = 80 — Pen: 22 Inches.

Very Ancient, Author and date unknown.

SIR FESTUS BURKE.

Maelz: ♩ = 84 — Pend. 18 Inches. 44. By CAROLAN.

THE PRINCESS ROYAL.
Mael: ♪ = 152 — Pen: 6 Inches:
45.
By CAROLAN.
Rather Slow and Moderately.
p
tr
f
p
✻ by License.

GRANU WEAL — or MA, MA, MA.
Mael: = 120 — Pen: 8 Inches.
46.
Very Ancient, Author and date unknown.
Rather Slow and Quietly.
ma, ma, ma.
ma, ma, ma.
ma, ma, ma.
ma, ma, ma.
ma, ma, ma.
ma, ma, ma.
ma, ma, ma.
KISS ME LADY.
Mael: = 152 — Pen: 6 Inches.
47.
Very Ancient, Author and date unknown.
Quick.

TAKE MY LOVE.
48.
Mael: ♪ = 100 — Pen: 10 Inches.
Author and date unknown.
With Spirit.
CELIA CONNALLON.
49.
Mael: ♪ = 100 — Pen: 12 Inches.
TOM CONNALLON 1650.
Rather Slow but Spirited.
tenuto
ten:
Very soft & slow
In 1st time.
At pleasure

WHY SHOULD NOT POOR FOLK.

Mael: ♩. = 108 — Pen: 10 Inches. 50. Author and date unknown.

Very piano

R.H. R.H.

GET UP EARLY.

51.

Mael: ♩. = 100 — Pen: 12 Inches.

Very Ancient, Author and date unknown.

Spirited. and Quick.

f

f

f p f

f p

THE TREE IN THE WOOD.
Mael: ♪ = 108 — Pen: 10 Inches.
52.
Very Ancient, Author and date unknown.
Rather Slow and Plaintive.
Softly.
f
Dim:
ppp
PRETTY BROWN MAID.
Mael: ♩. = 100 — Pen: 12 Inches.
53.
Very Ancient, Author and date unknown,
Brisk and Lively.
f

THE WHITE CALF.
Mael: = 96 — Pen: 14 Inches.
54.
Very Ancient, Author and date unknown.
A little Quick.
pp
THE REJECTED LOVER.
Mael: = 138 — Pen: 7 Inches.
55.
Author and date unknown.
Moderately Lively.
p
f
p
f
p
f
p
f

BALLINDERRY and CRONAN.

Mael: ♪ = 152 — Pen: 6 Inches. 56. Very Ancient, Author and date unknown.

THE GIRL I LEFT BEHIND ME
Mael: = 120 — Pen: 8 Inches.
57
Author and date unknown.
With tender expression.
p
f
p
PLANGSTY MISS BURKE.
Mael: = 100 — Pen: 12 Inches.
58.
By CAROLAN.
Gracefully and distinctly.
sf
sf
p
f

I CAN WEAVE LINEN.

Mael: ♩. = 96 — Pen: 14 Inches. **59.** Author and date unknown.

Lively but not Quick.

CHORUS.

ff

LOVE'S A TORMENTING PAIN.

Mael: ♩ = 108 — Pen: 10 Inches. **60.** W. CONNALLON 1670.

Tenderly and Gracefully.

tr

LADY BLANEY.

61.

Mael: ♪ = 96 — Pen: 14 Inches.

By CAROLAN.

MOLLY MY TREASURE.

ff
PLANGSTY HUGH O'DONNELL
Mael: = 120 — Pen: 8 Inches.
64.
By CAROLAN.
Quick.
f
p
ff

THE ROBBER — or CHARLEY REILLY.

Mael: ♪ = 96 — Pen: 14 Inches. **65.** Very Ancient, Author and date unknown.

A LITTLE HOUR BEFORE DAY.

Mael: ♪ = 108 — Pen 10 Inches. **66.** Very Ancient, Author and date unknown.

FANNY POWER

67.

Mael: 𝅗𝅥. =88 — Pen: 16 Inches.

By CAROLAN.

Distinctly and Gracefully.

MARY WITH THE FAIR LOCKS.

68.

Mael: 𝅘𝅥 = 100 — Pen: 12 Inches.

Very Ancient, Author and date unknown.

In moderate time.

p f p f p tr

CHARLES MACHUGH — THE WILD BOY.
Mael: ♪ = 108 — Pen: 10 Inches.
69.
Very Ancient, Author and date unknown
Slow and Tenderly.
DIRTY JAMES.
Mael: ♩. = 108 — Pen: 10 Inches.
70.
Author and date unknown
Very Quick.

THE WHITE BLANKET.

71.

Mael: ♪ = 188 — Pen: 7 Inches.

Very Ancient, Author and date unknown

Rather Slow and Distinctly.

THERE WAS A YOUNG LADY.

Mael: ♪ = 152 — Pen: 6 Inches. **72.** **Very Ancient, Author** and date unknown.

In moderate time.

CAROLAN'S DEVOTION

73.

Mael: ♪ = 96 — Pen: 14 Inches. Compd. about 1700.

⁜ by License.

CONSIDER THE STORY.
Mael: ♩. = 80 — Pen: 20 Inches.
74.
Author and date unknown.
Quick and Fiercely.
Och hone
1st
2nd
Och hone
Play over again at pleasure.
CAROLAN'S RECEIPT — or STAFFORD'S RECEIPT FOR WHISKEY.
Mael: ♩ = 96 — Pen: 14 Inches.
75.
Compd. about 1725.
Gracefully and Moderately Quick.
p
tr
pp

SWEET PORTAFERRY.

76.

Mael: ♪ = 152 — Pen: 6 Inches.

Very Ancient, Author and date unknown.

Tenderly and Plaintive.

p *f* *p* *f* *p* *f* *p* *f*

THE YELLOW BITTERN.

Mael: ♪ = 152 — Pen: 6 Inches. 77. Very Ancient, Author and date unknown.

SOFT MILD MORNING.

78.

Mael: ♩ = 108 — Pen: 10 Inches. Very Ancient, Author and date unknown.

THE YELLOW BLANKET.
Mael: ♩ = 108 — Pen: 10 Inches.
79.
Very Ancient, Author and date unknown.
Soft and Plaintive but not Slow.
O' DONNELL'S MARCH.
Mael: ♩. = 88 — Pen: 16 Inches.
80.
Very Ancient, Author and date unknown.
Lively and Spirited.

IRISH CRY

AS SUNG IN ULSTER.

81.

Mael: ♩ = 104 — Pen: 11 Inches. Very Ancient, Author and date unknown.

The Goll.

Second Goll and half Chorus.

8va alta
With great Animation.
fff
PED:
*
PED:
Dim:
p
Cres:
Dim:
Cres:
PED:
Cres:
Dim:
PED:
ppp
*
PED:
to be repeated.

Half Chorus of Sighs and Tears.

THE BEGGARMAN.

82.

HEALTH FROM THE CUP

DERMOT AND HIS LASS.

86.

Mael: ♪ = 92 — Pen: 15 Inches. Very Ancient, Author and date unknown.

Rather Slow and Plaintive.

I DO NOT INCLINE.

87.

Mael: ♩. = 80. — Pen: 20 Inches. Author and date unknown.

Briskly.

KATTY QUIN.
Mael: ♩ = 108. — Pen: 10 Inches.
88.
Very Ancient, Author and date unknown.
Moderately Quick.
THE PRETTY RED GIRL.
Mael: ♩ = 152 — Pen: 6 Inches.
89.
Very Ancient, Author and date unknown.
Spirited and Quick.

LITTLE MOLLY O!

Mael: ♩ = 100 — Pen: 12 Inches. **90.** Very Ancient, Author and date unknown.

Distinctly.

PATRICK'S DAY.

Mael: ♩. = 138 — Pen: 7 Inches. **91.** Author and date unknown.

Quick.

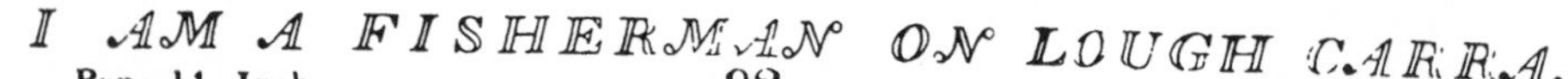

I AM A FISHERMAN ON LOUGH CARRA.

Mael: ♩ = 96 — Pen: 14 Inches. 92.

Very Ancient, Author and date unknown.

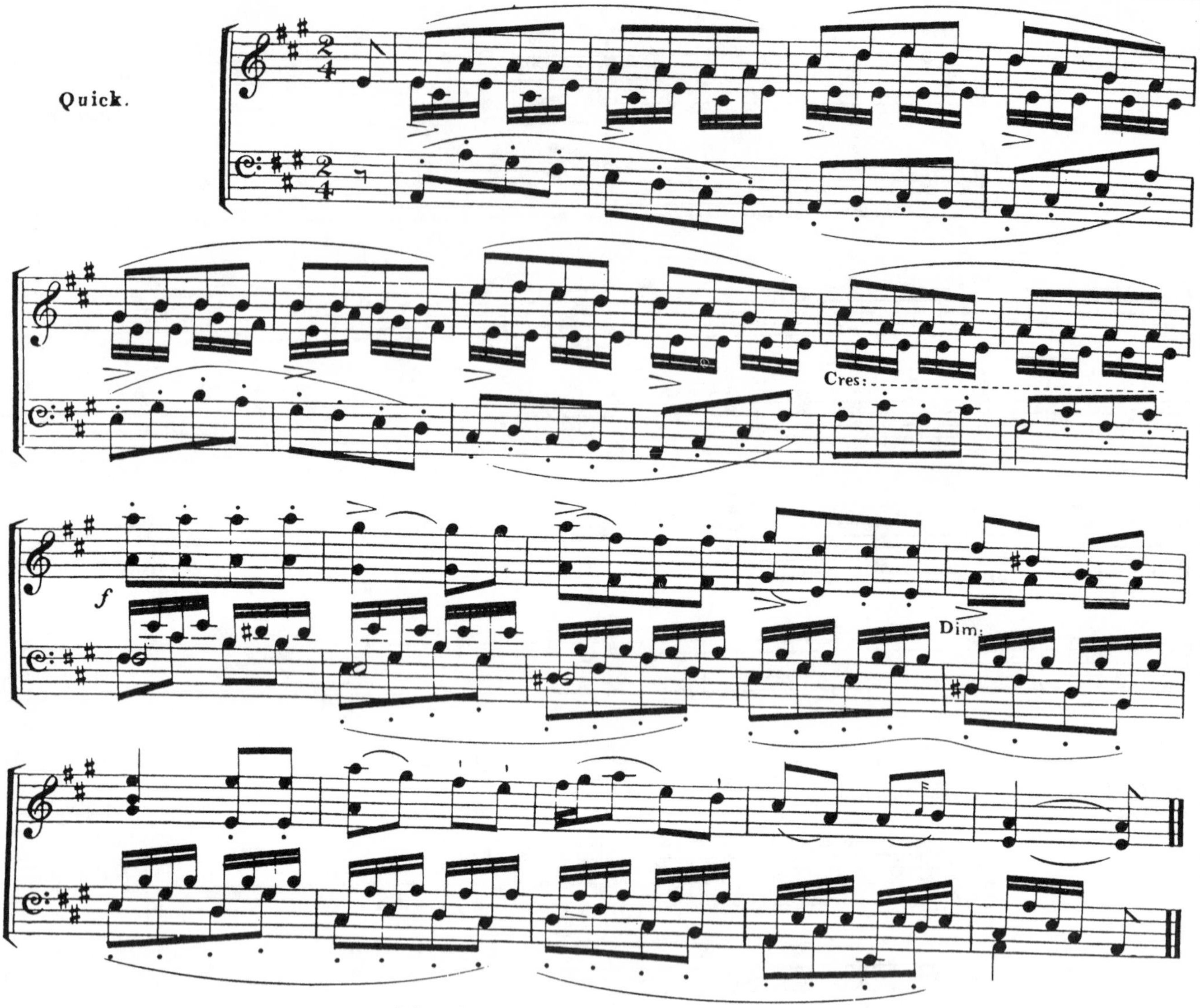

Quick.
Cres:
f
Dim:

MADAM MAXWELL.

Mael: ♩ = 96 — Pen: 14 Inches. 93.

By CAROLAN.

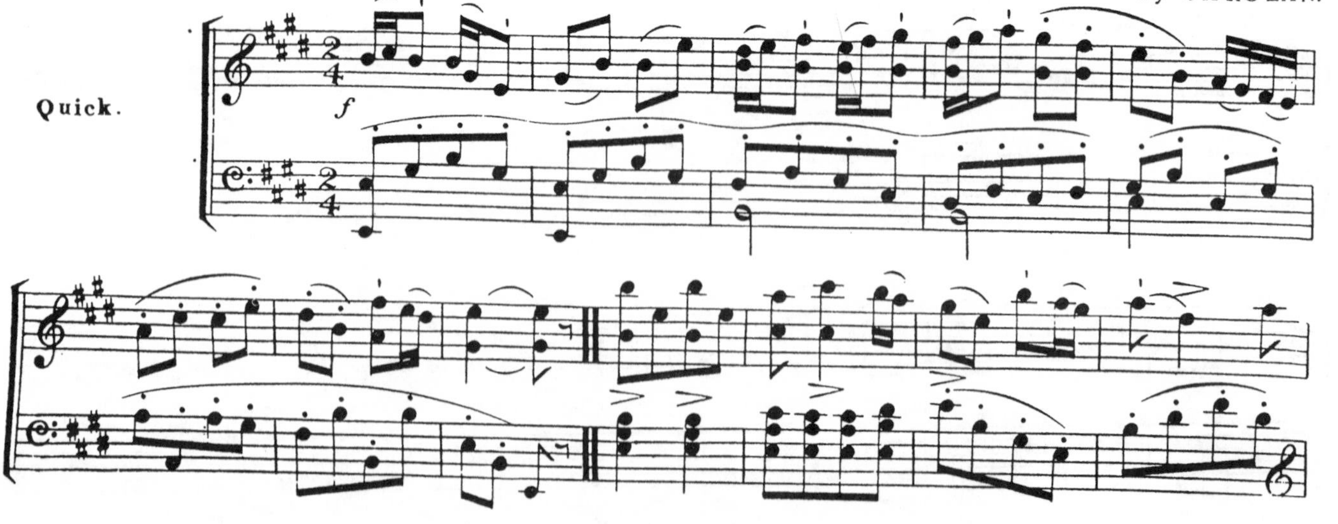

Quick.
f

'TIS A PITY I DON'T SEE MY LOVE.
Mael: ♩. = 80 — Pen: 20 Inches.
94.
Very Ancient, Author and date unknown.
Gracefully and Distinctly.
tr
f

THE LITTLE SWALLOW.

Mael: ♪ = 120 — Pen: 8 Inches. 95. Very Ancient, Author and date unknown.

Cronan.
Very softly
I AM A POOR & RAMBLING BOY.
Mael: ♪ = 108 — Pen: 10 Inches.
96.
Very Ancient, Author and date unknown.
Plaintive and Slow.
pp
KITTY NOWLAN.
Mael: ♩ = 88 — Pen: 16 Inches.
97.
Very Ancient, Author and date unknown.
In moderate time.
p
ff
ppp

THE BLACKBIRD.

98.

Mael: ♪ = 152 — Pen: 6 Inches.

Very Ancient, Author and date unknown.

CLARA BURKE.

99.

Mael: ♪ = 96. — Pen: 14 Inches.

Very Ancient, Author and date unknown.

I AM ASLEEP, AND DON'T WAKEN ME.

Mael: ♪ = 88 — Pen: 16 ¼ Inches. 100. Very Ancient, Author and date unknown.

Distinctly and moderately quick.

ff ten: ten: Dim: ten: pp f pp p ten: ten: ten:

ten:
ten:
Cres:
pp
BLACK HEADED DEARY.
101.
Mael: = 120 — Pen: 8 Inches.
Very Ancient, Author and date unknown.
Moderately Quick.
Dim:
Ped:
sf
CHORUS.
ten:
ff

THE MINERS OF WICKLOW.

Mael: ♩. = 152 — Pen: 6 Inches.

102.

Author and date unknown.

Very Quick and Animated.

CHORUS JIG.

Mael: ♩ = 88 — Pen: 16 Inches.

103.

Author and date unknown.

Spirited and Distinctly.

EMON DODWELL.
104.
Mael: = 120 — Pen; 8 Inches.
By CAROLAN, About 1698.
With Spirit.
p
tr
f
Cres:
Dim:
p
pp
THE DARLING.
105.
Mael: = 108 — Pen: 12 Inches.
Very Ancient, Author and date unknown.
Rather Slow and Gracefully.
pp
tr
pp
f
ff
p
tr

THE DEAF OLD MAN.

106.

Mael: ♪ = 120 — Pen: 8 Inches.

Very Ancient, Author and date unknown.

MISS HAMILTON.

107.

Mael: ♩ = 84 — Pen: 18 Inches. By LYONS in 1706.

BONNY PORTMORE.

Mael: ♪ = 96 — Pen: 13 Inches. **109.** Very Ancient, Author and date unknown.

Cres?
Dim?
ppp
Dim?
THE CUCKOO'S NEST
Mael: = 108 — Pen: 12 Inches.
110.
Author and date unknown.
Lively.
f
pp
f
p
f
pp

YOUNG BRIDGET.

MAC DONNELL'S MARCH.

Mael: ♩. = 120 — Pen: 8 Inches.

112.

Author and date unknown.

THE WILD GEESE.

Mael: ♩ = 92 — Pen 15 Inches. 113. Very Ancient, Author and date unknown.

pp
THE CONNAUGHT DAISY.
Mael: = 80 — Pen: 20 Inches.
114.
Author and date unknown.
In a lively manner.
p
f
p
Dolce
Cres?
tr
Dim?
f

SLIGO TUNE.

Mael: ♪ = 100 — Pen: 12 Inches. 115. Very Ancient, Author and date unknown.

Very Plaintive.

IS IT THE PRIEST YOU WANT?

Mael: ♩. = 108. — Pen: 10 Inches. 116. Very Ancient, Author and date unknown.

Lively and Quick.

SLOAN'S LAMENTATION.
Mæl: = 138 — Pen: 7 Inches.
117.
Very Ancient, Author and date unknown.
Rather Slow.
f
p
O! MOLLY DEAR.
Mæl: = 152 — Pen: 6 Inches.
118.
Very Ancient, Author and date unknown.
In moderate time.
p

COOLIN, OR LADY OF THE DESERT.

119.

Mael: ♪ = 104 — Pen: 11 Inches.

Very Ancient, Author and date unknown.
With Vars by LYONS in the year 1702.

VAR: 1st
A little quicker.
f
p
pp
f
VAR: 2nd
Slow and Plaintive.
Very soft.
tr
ten:

VAR: 3rd Quick and lively.
ten:
VAR: 4th Slower.
Very soft.
ten:

CARRICKMACROSS AIR
Mael: ♪ = 152 — Pen: 6 Inches.
120.
Very Ancient, Author and date unknown
Rather Slow and Pensive.
CELIA CONNALLON — SECOND SET.
Mael: ♪ = 100 — Pen: 12 Inches.
121.
TOM CONNALLON 1650.
Rather Slow.

COOEE EN DEVENISH, or THE LAMENTATION of YOUTHS.

Mael: 𝅘𝅥𝅮 = 100 — Pen: 10 Inches.

122.

Composed by HARRY SCOTT in 1603, for HUSSEY, Baron of Galtrim.

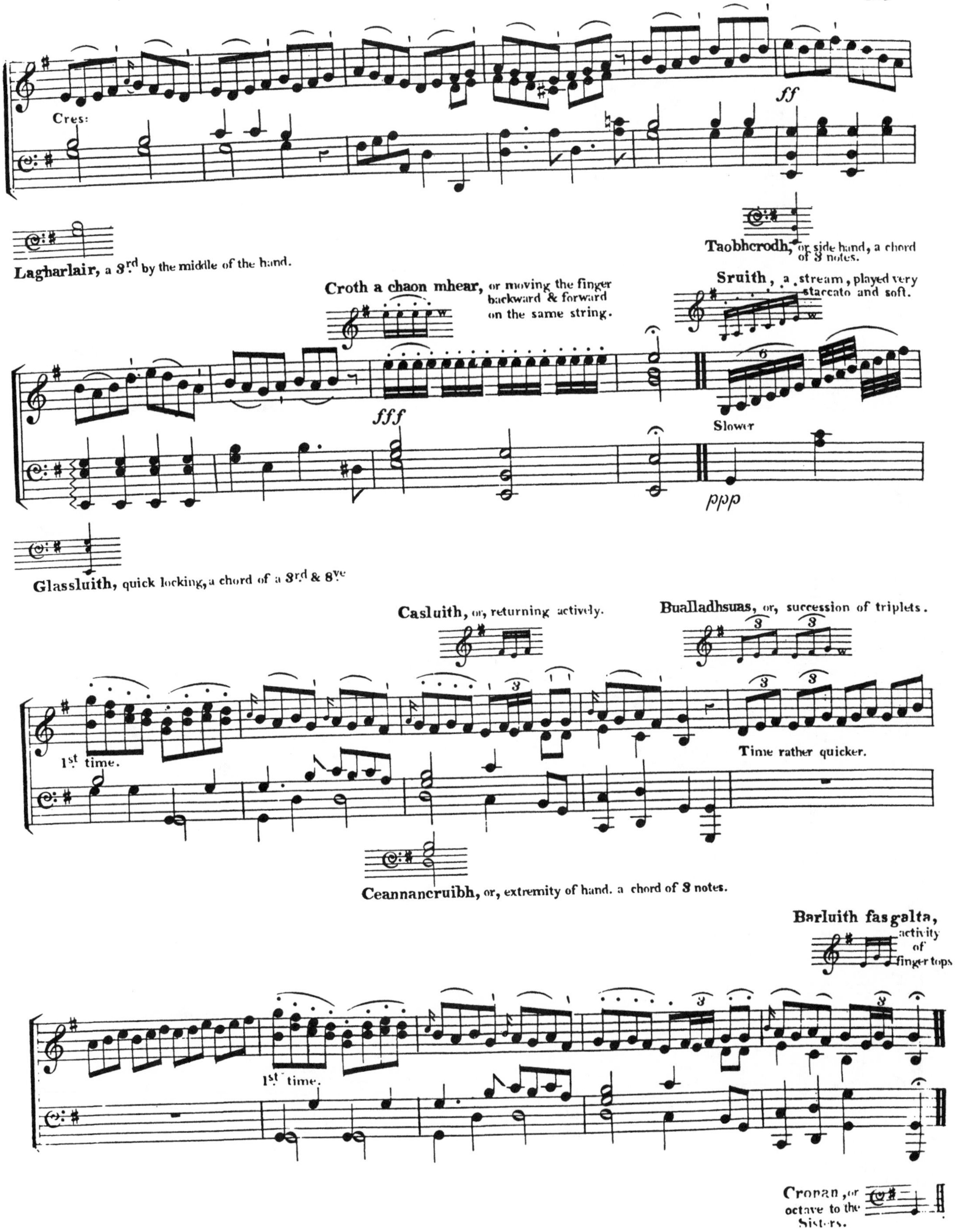

Cres:

ff

Lagharlair, a 3.rd by the middle of the hand.

Taobhcrodh, or side hand, a chord of 3 notes.

Croth a chaon mhear, or moving the finger backward & forward on the same string.

Sruith, a stream, played very staccato and soft.

fff

Slower

ppp

Glassluith, quick locking, a chord of a 3.rd & 8.ve

Casluith, or, returning actively.

Bualladhsuas, or, succession of triplets.

1.st time.

Time rather quicker.

Ceannancruibh, or, extremity of hand. a chord of 3 notes.

Barluith fasgalta, activity of finger tops

1.st time.

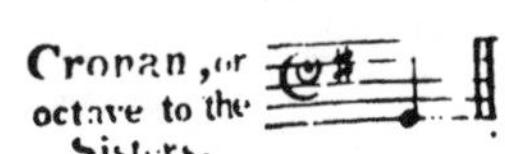

ELLEN A ROONE.

Mael: ♩ = 80 — Pen: 20 Inches. 123. Very Ancient, Author and date unknown.
Varied by LYONS in 1702.

JACKSON'S MORNING BRUSH.

Mael: ♩. = 152 — Pen 6 Inches. 124. Composed by JACKSON about 1776.

Lively and Animated.

THE BONNY CUCKOO.

Mael: ♪ = 144 — Pen: 6 Inches. **125.** Very Ancient, Author and date unknown.

Chearful and tenderly.

My Bonny Cuckoo I tell thee true That through the groves I'll rove with you I'll rove with you un...till the next spring And then my Cuckoo shall sweet..ly sing Cuc...koo Cuc..koo un...till the next spring And then my Cuc..koo shall sweet..ly sing.

The Ash and the Hazel shall mourning say,
My bonny Cuckoo dont go away,
Dont go away but tarry here,
And make the season last all the year.

PLOUGHMAN'S WHISTLE (Queen's County.)

Mael: ♪ = 116 — Pen: 10 Inches. **126.** Very Ancient, Author and date unknown.

Slow and Plaintive.

Play this an Octave lower at pleasure.

TOBY PEYTON'S PLANGSTY.
Mael: ♩. = 84. — Pen: 17 Inches.
127.
By CAROLAN.
Brisk and Lively.
THE COUNTY TYRONE.
Mael: ♪ = 76 — Pen: 19 Inches.
128.
Author and date unknown.
Rather Slow.
Bass very piano all through.

THE LITTLE BOLD FOX.
Mael: ♪ = 126 — Pen: 8 Inches.
129.
Very Ancient, Author and date unknown.
With life and spirit.
p
f
Soft.
f
CHORUS.
p
Very Loud.
THE LITTLE POT.
Mael: ♩ = 116 — Pen: 10 Inches.
130.
Author and date unknown.
In a playful manner.
tr
f
p

THE HURLER'S MARCH (King's County.)

Mael: ♪. = 116 — Pen: 10 Inches. **131.** Very Ancient, Author and date unknown.

With Life and Spirit.

THE BROWN AND WHITE GARLAND.

Mael: ♪ = 116 — Pen: 10 Inches. **132.** Very Ancient, Author and date unknown.

IF I HAD A COURT AND CASTLE.

Mael: ♩ = 108 — Pen: 12 Inches. **133.** Author and date unknown.

SPINNING WHEEL SONGS.

Mael: 𝅘𝅥𝅮. = 84 — Pen: 17 Inches. 134. Very Ancient, Author and date unknown.

PLOUGHMAN'S WHISTLE.

137.

Mael: ♪ = 116 — Pen: 10 Inches

Very Ancient, Author and date unknown.

This may be played an Octave lower with good effect.

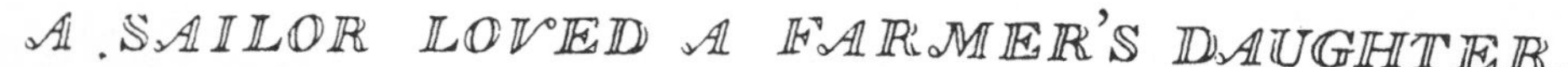

A SAILOR LOVED A FARMER'S DAUGHTER.

Mael: ♪ = 116 — Pen: 10 Inches. 138. Very Ancient, Author and date unknown.

In a graceful style.

O! WHITE MAIVE.

Mael: ♩ = 69 — Pen: 24 Inches. 139. Very Ancient, Author and date unknown.

Slow and mournful.

THE WILD COLT.
140.
Mael: ♩. = 100 — Pen: 14 Inches.
Author and date unknown.
With animation.
p
f
p
p
f
I WILL PAY THEM YET.
141.
Mael: ♩. = 84 — Pen: 16 Inches.
Author and date unknown.
With Spirit.

A LOVELY LASS TO A FRIAR CAME.

Mael: ♪ = 126 — Pen: 8 Inches. 142. Very Ancient, Author and date unknown.
The Var: by LYONS in 1698.

THE PHARROH or WAR MARCH.

O'REILLY'S LAMENTATION.

Mael: ♪ = 116 — Pen: 10 Inches.

144.

Very Ancient, Author & date unknown.

Rather Slow and Plaintive.

pp *f* *pp* *f* *pp*

ACHIL AIR.

Mael: ♩ = 88 — Pen: 16 Inches.

145.

Very Ancient, Author & date unknown.

Very Plaintive.

f *tr* *p* *f* *b tr*

THE HARE IN THE CORN.

Mael: ♩. = 116 — Pen: 10 Inches. **146.** Author and date unknown.

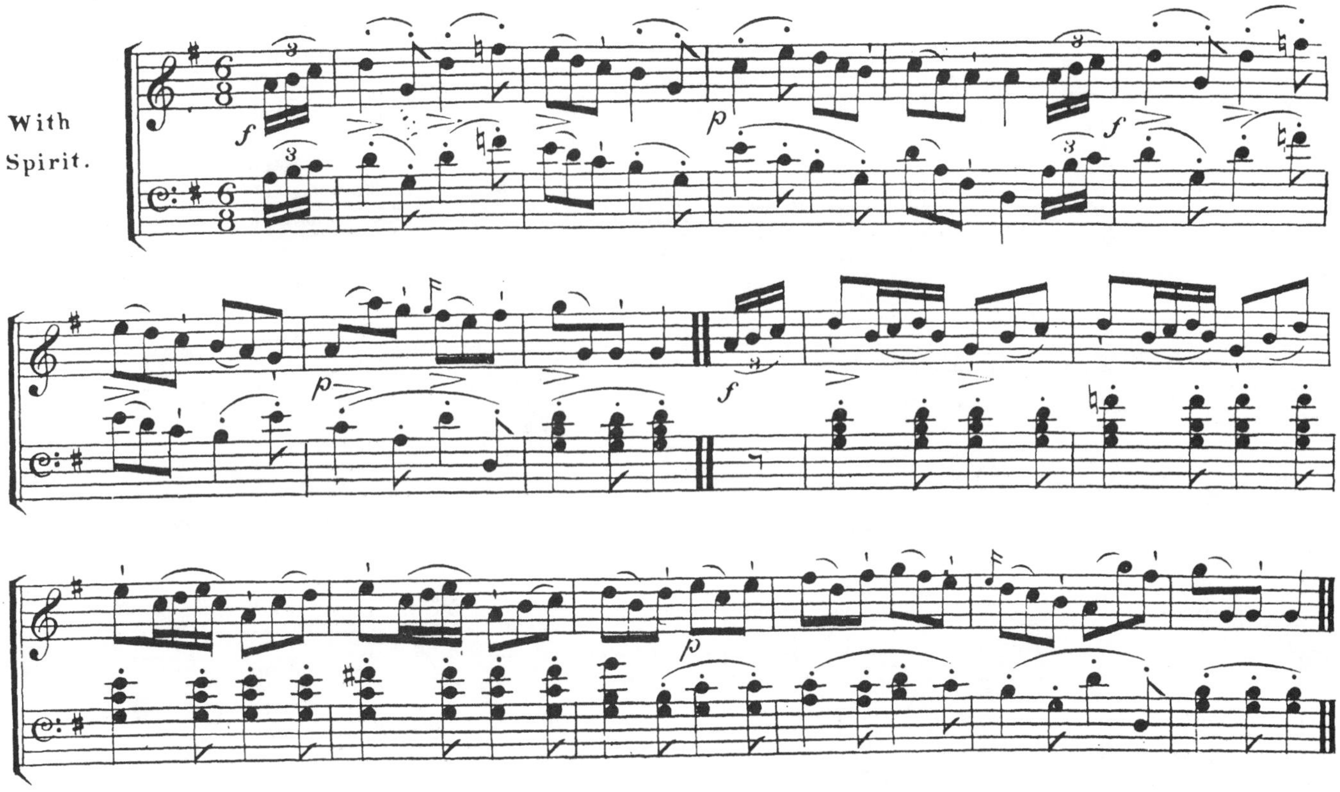

With Spirit.

THE CHANTER'S TUNE.

Mael: ♪ = 116 — Pen: 10 Inches. **147.** Author and date unknown.

A little slow and distinctly.

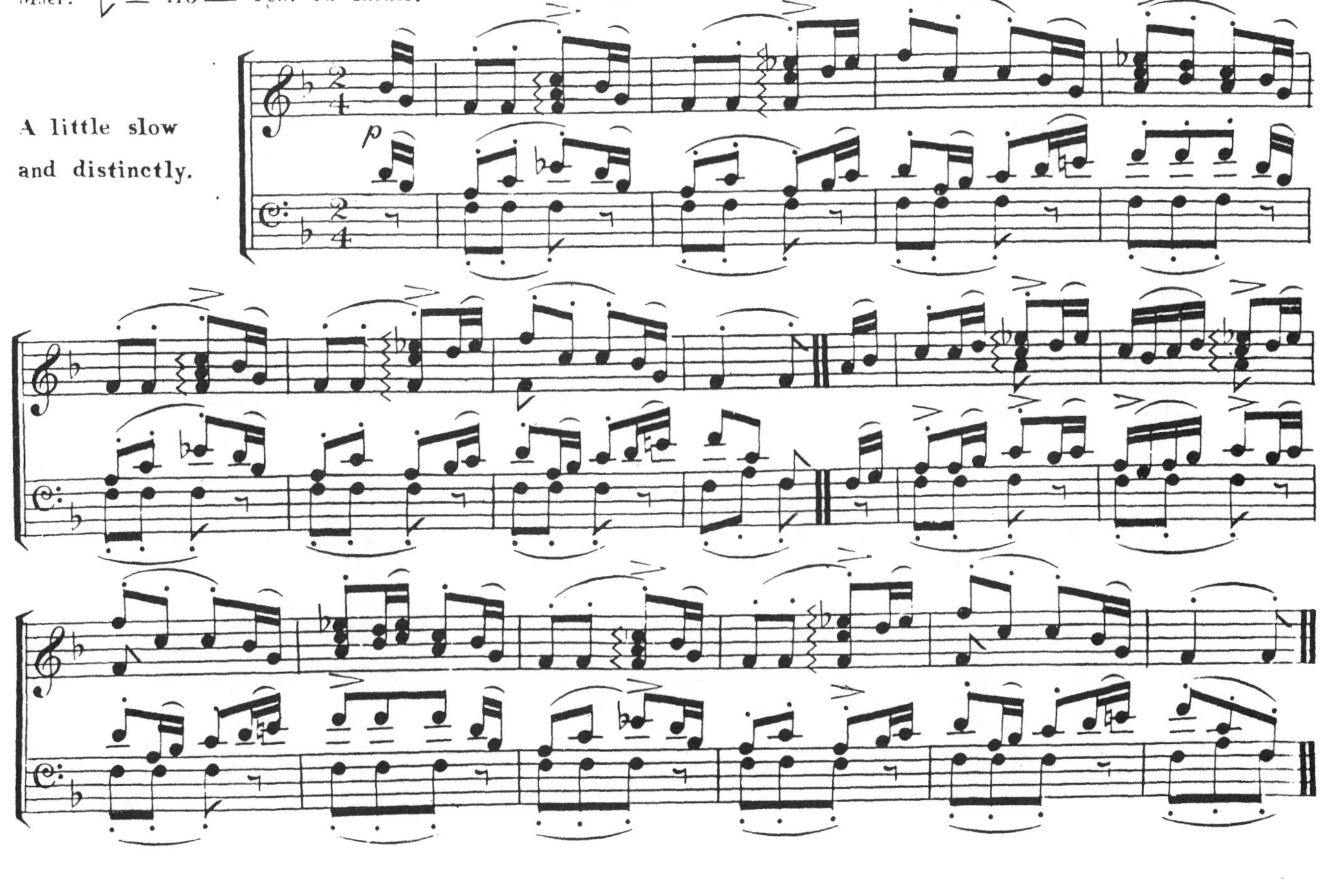

THE GENTLE MAIDEN.

THE FOGGY DEW.

150.

Maelz = 108 — Pen: 12 Inches.

Very Ancient, Author and date unknown.

With Spirit.

p f pp f p f

IRISH JIGG

151.

Maelz = 144 — Pen: 6 Inches.

Very Ancient, Author and date unknown.

With great animation.

Finis.

London. Engraved by R.T. SKARRATT, 5 Eyre Street, Hatton Garden.

END OF THE DOVER EDITION

Dover Popular Songbooks

"FOR ME AND MY GAL" AND OTHER FAVORITE SONG HITS, 1915–1917, David A. Jasen (ed.). 31 great hits: Pretty Baby, MacNamara's Band, Over There, Old Grey Mare, Beale Street, M-O-T-H-E-R, more, with original sheet music covers, complete vocal and piano. 144pp. 9 × 12. 28127-2 Pa. **$9.95**

POPULAR IRISH SONGS, Florence Leniston (ed.). 37 all-time favorites with vocal and piano arrangements: "My Wild Irish Rose," "Irish Eyes are Smiling," "Last Rose of Summer," "Danny Boy," many more. 160pp. 26755-5 Pa. **$9.95**

FAVORITE SONGS OF THE NINETIES, edited by Robert Fremont. 88 favorites: "Ta-Ra-Ra-Boom-De-Aye," "The Band Played on," "Bird in a Gilded Cage," etc. 401pp. 9 × 12. 21536-9 Pa. **$17.95**

POPULAR SONGS OF NINETEENTH-CENTURY AMERICA, edited by Richard Jackson. 64 most important songs: "Old Oaken Bucket," "Arkansas Traveler," "Yellow Rose of Texas," etc. 290pp. 9 × 12. 23270-0 Pa. **$14.95**

SONG HITS FROM THE TURN OF THE CENTURY, edited by Paul Charosh, Robert A. Fremont. 62 big hits: "Silver Heels," "My Sweetheart's the Man in the Moon," etc. 296pp. 9 × 12. (Except British Commonwealth [but may be sold in Canada]) 23158-5 Pa. **$8.95**

ALEXANDER'S RAGTIME BAND AND OTHER FAVORITE SONG HITS, 1901–1911, edited by David A. Jasen. Fifty vintage popular songs America still sings, reprinted in their entirety from the original editions. Introduction. 224pp. 9 × 12. (Available in U.S. only) 25331-7 Pa. **$14.95**

"PEG O' MY HEART" AND OTHER FAVORITE SONG HITS, 1912 & 1913, edited by Stanley Appelbaum. 36 songs by Berlin, Herbert, Handy and others, with complete lyrics, full piano arrangements and original sheet music covers in black and white. 176pp. 9 × 12. 25998-6 Pa. **$12.95**

SONGS OF THE CIVIL WAR, Irwin Silber (ed.). Piano, vocal, guitar chords for 125 songs including *Battle Cry of Freedom, Marching Through Georgia, Dixie, Oh, I'm a Good Old Rebel, The Drummer Boy of Shiloh,* many more. 400pp. 8⅜ × 11. 28438-7 Pa. **$16.95**

AMERICAN BALLADS AND FOLK SONGS, John A. Lomax and Alan Lomax. Over 200 songs, music and lyrics: *Frankie and Albert, John Henry, Frog Went a-Courtin', Down in the Valley, Skip to My Lou,* other favorites. Notes on each song. 672pp. 5⅜ × 8½. 28276-7 Pa. **$13.95**

"TAKE ME OUT TO THE BALL GAME" AND OTHER FAVORITE SONG HITS, 1906–1908, edited by Lester Levy. 23 favorite songs from the turn-of-the-century with lyrics and original sheet music covers: "Cuddle Up a Little Closer, Lovey Mine," "Harrigan," "Shine on, Harvest Moon," "School Days," other hits. 128pp. 9 × 12. 24662-0 Pa. **$9.95**

THE AMERICAN SONG TREASURY: 100 Favorites, edited by Theodore Raph. Complete piano arrangements, guitar chords and lyrics for 100 best-loved tunes, "Buffalo Gals," "Oh, Suzanna," "Clementine," "Camptown Races," and much more. 416pp. 8⅛ × 11. 25222-1 Pa. **$15.95**

"THE ST. LOUIS BLUES" AND OTHER SONG HITS OF 1914, edited by Sandy Marrone. Full vocal and piano for "By the Beautiful Sea," "Play a Simple Melody," "They Didn't Believe Me," 21 songs in all. 112pp. 9 × 12. 26383-5 Pa. **$9.95**

STEPHEN FOSTER SONG BOOK, Stephen Foster. 40 favorites: "Beautiful Dreamer," "Camptown Races," "Jeanie with the Light Brown Hair," "My Old Kentucky Home," etc. 224pp. 9 × 12. 23048-1 Pa. **$10.95**

ONE HUNDRED ENGLISH FOLKSONGS, edited by Cecil J. Sharp. Border ballads, folksongs, collected from all over Great Britain. "Lord Bateman," "Henry Martin," "The Green Wedding," many others. Piano. 235pp. 9 × 12. 23192-5 Pa. **$14.95**

THE CIVIL WAR SONGBOOK, edited by Richard Crawford. 37 songs: "Battle Hymn of the Republic," "Drummer Boy of Shiloh," "Dixie," 34 more. 157pp. 9 × 12. 23422-3 Pa. **$9.95**

SONGS OF WORK AND PROTEST, Edith Fowke, Joe Glazer. 100 important songs: "Union Maid," "Joe Hill," "We Shall Not Be Moved," many more. 210pp. 7⅞ × 10¾. 22899-1 Pa. **$10.95**

A RUSSIAN SONG BOOK, edited by Rose N. Rubin and Michael Stillman. 25 traditional folk songs, plus 19 popular songs by twentieth-century composers. Full piano arrangements, guitar chords. Lyrics in original Cyrillic, transliteration and English translation. With discography. 112p. 9 × 12. 26118-2 Pa. **$8.95**

FAVORITE CHRISTMAS CAROLS, selected and arranged by Charles J. F. Cofone. Title, music, first verse and refrain of 34 traditional carols in handsome calligraphy; also subsequent verses and other information in type. 79pp. 8⅜ × 11. 20445-6 Pa. **$4.95**

SEVENTY SCOTTISH SONGS, Helen Hopekirk (ed.). Complete piano and vocals for classics of Scottish song: *Flow Gently, Sweet Afton, Comin' thro' the Rye (Gin a Body Meet a Body), The Campbells are Comin', Robin Adair,* many more. 208pp. 8⅜ × 11. 27029-7 Pa. **$12.95**

35 SONG HITS BY GREAT BLACK SONGWRITERS: Bert Williams, Eubie Blake, Ernest Hogan and Others, David A. Jasen (ed.). Ballads, show tunes, other early 20th-century works by black songwriters include "Some of These Days," "A Good Man Is Hard to Find," "I'm Just Wild About Harry," "Love Will Find a Way," 31 other classics. Reprinted from rare sheet music, original covers. 160pp. 9 x 12. (USO) 40416-1 Pa. **$12.95**

"BEALE STREET" AND OTHER CLASSIC BLUES: 38 Works, 1901–1921, David A. Jasen (ed.). "St. Louis Blues," "The Hesitating Blues," "Down Home Blues," "Jelly Roll Blues," "Railroad Blues," and many more. Reproduced directly from rare sheet music (including original covers). Introduction. 160pp. 9 x 12. (USO) 40183-9 Pa. **$12.95**

"A PRETTY GIRL IS LIKE A MELODY" AND OTHER FAVORITE SONG HITS, 1918–1919, David A. Jasen (ed.). "After You've Gone," "How Ya Gonna Keep 'Em Down on the Farm," "I'm Always Chasing Rainbows," "Rock-a-Bye Your Baby" and 36 other Golden Oldies. 176pp. 9 x 12. 29421-8 Pa. **$12.95**

500 BEST-LOVED SONG LYRICS, Ronald Herder (ed.). Complete lyrics for well-known folk songs, hymns, popular and show tunes, more. "Oh Susanna," "The Battle Hymn of the Republic," "When Johnny Comes Marching Home," hundreds more. Indispensable for singalongs, parties, family get-togethers, etc. 416pp. 5⅜ x 8½. 29725-X Pa. **$10.95**

MY FIRST BOOK OF AMERICAN FOLK SONGS: 20 Favorite Pieces in Easy Piano Arrangements, Bergerac (ed.). Expert settings of traditional favorites by a well-known composer and arranger for young pianists: *Amazing Grace, Blue Tail Fly, Sweet Betsy from Pike,* many more. 48pp. 8¼ x 11. 28885-4 Pa. **$3.95**

MY FIRST BOOK OF CHRISTMAS SONGS: 20 Favorite Songs in Easy Piano Arrangements, Bergerac (ed.). Beginners will love playing these beloved favorites in easy arrangements: "Jingle Bells," "Deck the Halls," "Joy to the World," "Silent Night," "Away in a Manger," "Hark! The Herald Angels Sing," 14 more. Illustrations. 48pp. 8¼ x 11. 29718-7 Pa. **$3.95**

*Available from your music dealer or write for **free** Music Catalog to*
Dover Publications, Inc., Dept. MUBI, 31 East 2nd Street, Mineola, N.Y. 11501.